W9-BJH-227

Crystallization-Study
of
Deuteronomy

Volume Two

Watchman Nee
Witness Lee

The Holy Word for Morning Revival

LUCY
6/5/20

Living Stream Ministry
Anaheim, CA • www.lsm.org

First Edition, February 2020.

ISBN 978-1-5360-0356-7

Published by

Living Stream Ministry
2431 W. La Palma Ave., Anaheim, CA 92801 U.S.A.
P. O. Box 2121, Anaheim, CA 92814 U.S.A.

Printed in the United States of America

20 21 22 / 4 3 2 1

2019 December Semiannual Training

**CRYSTALLIZATION-STUDY
OF DEUTERONOMY**

Contents

Preface

1. This book is intended as an aid to believers in developing a daily time of morning revival with the Lord in His word. At the same time, it provides a limited review of the semi-annual training held December 23-28, 2019, in Anaheim, California, on the "Crystallization-study of Deuteronomy." Through intimate contact with the Lord in His word, the believers can be constituted with life and truth and thereby equipped to prophesy in the meetings of the church unto the building up of the Body of Christ.

2. The book is divided into weeks. One training message is covered per week. Each week presents first the message outline, followed by six daily portions, a hymn, and then some space for writing. The training outline has been divided into days, corresponding to the six daily portions. Each daily portion covers certain points and begins with a section entitled "Morning Nourishment." This section contains selected verses and a short reading that can provide rich spiritual nourishment through intimate fellowship with the Lord. The "Morning Nourishment" is followed by a section entitled "Today's Reading," a longer portion of ministry related to the day's main points. Each day's portion concludes with a short list of references for further reading and some space for the saints to make notes concerning their spiritual inspiration, enlightenment, and enjoyment to serve as a reminder of what they have received of the Lord that day.

3. The space provided at the end of each week is for composing a short prophecy. This prophecy can be composed by considering all of our daily notes, the "harvest" of our inspirations during the week, and preparing a main point with some subpoints to be spoken in the church meetings for the organic building up of the Body of Christ.

4. Following the last week in this volume, we have provided reading schedules for both the Old and New Testaments in the Recovery Version with footnotes. These schedules are arranged so that one can read through both the Old and

New Testaments of the Recovery Version with footnotes in two years.

5. As a practical aid to the saints' feeding on the Word throughout the day, we have provided verse cards at the end of the volume, which correspond to each day's Scripture reading. These may be cut out and carried along as a source of spiritual enlightenment and nourishment in the saints' daily lives.

6. The content of this book is taken primarily from *Crystallization-study Outlines—Deuteronomy,* the text and footnotes of the Recovery Version of the Bible, selections from the writings of Witness Lee and Watchman Nee, and *Hymns,* all of which are published by Living Stream Ministry.

7. *Crystallization-study Outlines—Deuteronomy* was compiled by Living Stream Ministry from the writings of Witness Lee and Watchman Nee. The outlines, footnotes, and cross-references in the Recovery Version of the Bible are by Witness Lee. Unless otherwise noted, the references cited in this publication are by Witness Lee.

8. For the sake of space, references to *The Collected Works of Watchman Nee* and *The Collected Works of Witness Lee* are abbreviated to *CWWN* and *CWWL,* respectively.

CRYSTALLIZATION-STUDY
OF DEUTERONOMY

Key Statements:

God was leading His people into the good land,
a type of Christ, by Christ, and He was sustaining them
on their way to the good land also by Christ,
who is everything that proceeds out
through the mouth of God; every word in Deuteronomy
is the very Christ, who is now the word of God
for us to receive as our life and life supply.

The government of God
is the governmental administration
of the righteous, holy, faithful,
tender, loving, and compassionate God.

Because we are practically joined to Christ as
the reality of the good land and are enjoying His riches,
God's eyes are upon us continually,
causing us to enjoy God's presence
and making us the object of His care.

Those who are qualified to inherit and live
in the good land know God's heart
and God's government, love God, trust in God,
fear God, subject themselves to God's ruling,
mind the tender feelings of God,
and live in the presence of God.

At the entrance of the church there is the cross,
and in order to meet as the church,
we must experience the cross for the crucifying
of the self, for the overthrowing of "reasonings and
every high thing rising up against the knowledge
of God," and for the exalting of Christ alone
so that He may be all and in all for God's expression
and the unique testimony of oneness.

Believers in Christ who live under the government
of God choose life and receive blessing,
living according to the principle of life and realizing
that in the Christian life and the church life
everything depends on the Lord's blessing.

Christ—the True Prophet
Typified by Moses

Scripture Reading: Deut. 18:15-19; Acts 3:22-23

Day 1

I. **Prophets are God's spokesmen—Deut. 18:15; Amos 3:7; Isa. 6:1-8:**
   A. The function of the prophets is to speak for God— 1 Cor. 14:31; 2 Tim. 4:2.
   B. According to the Bible, the main function of a prophet is not to predict things that are coming but to speak for God and to speak forth God by God's revelation— Amos 3:7; Exo. 4:10-16.
   C. God, who is a speaking God, spoke in the Old Testament to people in many portions and in many ways in the prophets—Heb. 1:1:
      1. God is hidden, but through the speaking of the prophets, God Himself and His intention are made known—Isa. 45:15, 19; 1:1-2a; 6:1-8.
      2. Prophets receive God's revelation directly and are borne by the Spirit of God to speak for God and speak forth God—2 Pet. 1:20-21:
         a. No prophecy was ever borne by the will of man—v. 21.
         b. Man's will, desire, and wish, with his thought and exposition, were not the source from which any prophecy came.
         c. The source was God, by whose Holy Spirit men were borne, as a ship is borne by the wind, to speak out the will, desire, and wish of God.
         d. No prophecy of Scripture is of the prophet's or the writer's exposition, for no prophecy was ever borne, or carried along, by the will of man; rather, men spoke from God while being borne by the Spirit—vv. 20-21.

D. A false prophet is one who speaks a word presumptuously in God's name, which God did not command him to speak—Deut. 18:20-22.

Day 2

II. **Moses was a prophet, and as a prophet, he typifies Christ—v. 15:**

A. In his forty years of leading the children of Israel, Moses continually spoke to them for God; especially in Deuteronomy, Moses repeatedly spoke God's words to the children of Israel—1:1, 9-11, 18; 4:1-2; 5:11; 6:1-9.

B. Moses, as the spokesman of God, was like an aged, loving father speaking to his children with much love and concern—30:1-14:

1. Although it was Moses who spoke, he did not speak his own words; he spoke God's words—32:1-47.

2. He spoke for God, spoke forth God, and spoke God into the children of Israel—11:8-25.

C. Moses was a person not only soaked and saturated with the thought of God but also constituted with the speaking God Himself; therefore, the word that proceeded out of his mouth was the word of God spoken through this one spokesman—Exo. 34:29-35; Num. 12:6-8:

1. For forty years Moses served as God's spokesman, speaking for God, speaking forth God, and predicting; every word that he spoke became God's word—Deut. 10:12-22.

2. He predicted that the children of Israel would forsake God and be cast by God into all the nations but that when they would repent and turn to God, He would gather them from the nations—29:25-28; 30:1-3.

3. As such a prophet, Moses is a type of Christ—Acts 3:22-23.

4. Moses spoke to the children of Israel all that God had commanded him to speak; likewise, the

Lord Jesus spoke all that the Father commanded Him to speak—John 12:49-50.

Day 3

III. **The Old Testament prophet Moses prophesied, saying, "A Prophet will Jehovah your God raise up for you from your midst, from among your brothers, like me; you shall listen to Him"—Deut. 18:15:**

A. Jehovah would put His words in the mouth of the Prophet, who would speak all that God commanded Him—v. 18b.

B. The Prophet raised up by God would be according to all that the children of Israel asked of Jehovah their God at Horeb—vv. 16-17:

1. They had told Moses that they could not bear to hear God's voice—5:22-28; Exo. 20:18-19.

2. Because they wanted a prophet, Moses promised that God would fulfill their desire for a prophet.

C. Moses prophesied that Jehovah would raise up a Prophet from their midst, from among their brothers—Deut. 18:15, 18a:

1. This indicates that God would raise up this Prophet through the incarnation of Christ to speak the word of God—John 1:14; 3:34; 7:16-17; Heb. 1:2a.

2. *From the midst of their brothers* (Deut. 18:18a) indicates that Christ as the coming Prophet would be human as well as divine—John 1:1, 14; Rom. 8:3:

a. If Christ were merely God, He could not have been raised up from among the Israelites—Luke 1:31, 35.

b. As God, Christ could not be from among the Jews as a brother, but as the incarnated One, the One who put on human nature and was a Jew, Christ was from among His brothers.

c. As the incarnated God, Christ put on human nature and became a Jew; thus, He is the

Prophet raised up "from your midst," as prophesied by Moses—Deut. 18:15, 18.

   3. Acts 3:22-23 applies Deuteronomy 18:15-19 to
Christ, who is God incarnated to be a man, indi-
cating that Christ is the Prophet promised by
God to His people, the children of Israel.

IV. **In His first coming, Christ ministered as the
Prophet raised up by God—Acts 3:22-23; 7:37:**

  A. Through incarnation Christ became the Prophet
to speak the word of God—John 3:34.

  B. Christ is the Word of God and the speaking of God—
1:1; Rev. 19:13; Heb. 1:2a:

    1. When Christ was on the earth speaking for God
and teaching people, His teaching was not His
own but was according to what the Father had
taught Him—John 7:16; 8:28b.

    2. He did not speak from Himself; as the Father
spoke to Him, so He spoke—12:49-50.

    3. As God's Prophet, Christ spoke for God, spoke
forth God, and revealed God to the disciples—
Matt. 11:27.

  C. During His earthly ministry, Christ also prophesied, predicted, by declaring the things that are coming—John 16:12-13; Matt. 24:2—25:46.

  D. Today Christ as the Prophet is in us still speaking
for God to reveal God and speaking God into people—Rom. 8:10; 2 Cor. 13:5; Col. 1:27.

Day 4

V. **As a prophet typifying Christ as the true Prophet,
Moses might have spoken something of his own
feeling, but even this became the word of God; his
speaking in Deuteronomy was like Paul's speaking in 1 Corinthians 7:**

  A. Because Paul was a man constituted with God, his
opinion became a part of God's word as the divine
revelation in the New Testament:

    1. In his speaking, Paul was one with God; therefore,
what he spoke was God's speaking—6:17; 7:25.

    2. The principle is the same with Moses' speaking in Deuteronomy.

B. First Corinthians 7 conveys the spirit of a person who loves the Lord, who cares for the Lord's interests on earth, who is absolutely for the Lord and one with the Lord, and who in every respect is obedient, submissive, and satisfied with God and the circumstances arranged by Him.

Day 5 & Day 6

C. Because Paul was one with the Lord, when he spoke, the Lord spoke with him; thus, in 1 Corinthians 7 we have an example of the New Testament principle of incarnation—vv. 10, 12, 25, 40:

    1. The principle of incarnation is that God enters into man and mingles Himself with man to make man one with Himself; thus, God is in man, and man is in God—John 15:4-5.

    2. In the New Testament the Lord becomes one with His apostles, and they become one with Him and speak together with Him; thus, His word becomes their word, and whatever they utter is His word—1 Cor. 2:12-13.

    3. The principle in 1 Corinthians 7:10 is the same as that in Galatians 2:20, the principle of incarnation—two persons living as one person.

    4. In 1 Corinthians 7:25 and 40 we see the highest spirituality—the spirituality of a person who is so one with the Lord and permeated with Him that even his opinion expresses the Lord's mind.

    5. If we are saturated with the Spirit, what we express will be our thought, but it will also be something of the Lord because we are one with Him; this is the experience of Christ as the Prophet living in us to speak for God and to speak forth God—6:17.

Morning Nourishment

Amos Surely the Lord Jehovah will not do anything
3:7 unless He reveals His secret to His servants the
  prophets.
2 Pet. Knowing this first, that no prophecy of Scripture
1:20-21 is of one's own interpretation; for no prophecy
  was ever borne by the will of man, but men spoke
  from God while being borne by the Holy Spirit.

Prophets are God's spokesmen. They speak for God and speak forth God; sometimes they also predict. According to the Bible, the main function of a prophet is not to predict the things to come but to speak for God. For example, in Exodus 3 and 4 when Moses was called by God, he told God that he was slow of speech and of a slow tongue (4:10). So God gave Aaron to Moses to be his prophet (4:14-16; 7:1). Aaron did not predict for Moses; rather, he spoke for him. In the whole Bible, to prophesy is mainly to speak for God and to speak forth God; sometimes it is also to predict. To predict, however, is secondary. This is the proper meaning of prophesying in the Bible. (*Truth Lessons—Level One,* vol. 2, p. 19)

Today's Reading

[In 2 Peter 1:20] *one's* refers to the prophet who spoke the prophecy or the writer who wrote the prophecy. Literally, the Greek word for *interpretation* means loosening, untying; hence, disclosure, exposition, solution. *One's own interpretation* means the prophet's or writer's own exposition or solution, which is not inspired by God through the Holy Spirit. Peter's thought here is that no prophecy of Scripture is of the prophet's or writer's own concept, idea, or understanding; that no prophecy comes from that source, the source of man; that no prophecy originates from the private and personal thought of any prophet or writer. This is confirmed and explained by the following verse.

For [in verse 21] gives the explanation of the preceding verse. No prophecy of Scripture is of the prophet's or writer's solution, for no prophecy was ever borne or carried along by the will of man, but men spoke from God, being borne by the Holy Spirit.

The Greek word translated "borne" also means carried along. The same word is used in verses 17 and 18. No prophecy was ever carried along by the will of man. Man's will, desire, and wish, with his thought and solution, are not the source from which any prophecy came. The source is God, by whose Holy Spirit men were carried along, as a ship by the wind, to speak out the will, desire, and wish of God.

Because the prophets were carried along by the Holy Spirit, what they uttered was not of their own interpretation or will. On the contrary, what they spoke was the will of God, the concept of God uttered by a prophet who was carried along by the Holy Spirit.

Verses 20 and 21 prove that the prophetic word is altogether reliable and trustworthy. The prophecy in the Scriptures did not come from man's opinion. This prophecy is God's word, God's speaking. For this reason, we should believe whatever is prophesied in the Old Testament. Peter seems to be saying here, "The prophecy in the Bible is genuinely of God. Therefore, it is trustworthy. Do not listen to the heretical teachings of the apostates, of those who have deviated from the track of divine truth. Instead, you should give heed to the prophecies of the Old Testament and also hold to our testimony." (*Life-study of 2 Peter*, pp. 73-74)

Deuteronomy 18:20-22 concerns the false prophet. A false prophet was one who spoke a word presumptuously in God's name which God did not command him to speak or who spoke in the name of other gods (v. 20a). Such a prophet was to be put to death (v. 20b). When a prophet spoke in the name of Jehovah and the thing did not happen, that was the thing which Jehovah had not spoken (v. 22). (*Life-study of Deuteronomy*, pp. 141-142)

Further Reading: Truth Lessons—Level One, vol. 2, lsn. 14;
Life-study of 2 Peter, msg. 8

Enlightenment and inspiration:_____

_____

_____

_____

Morning Nourishment

Deut. A Prophet will Jehovah your God raise up for
18:15 you from your midst, from among your brothers, like me; you shall listen to Him.
   18 A Prophet will I raise up for them from the midst
of their brothers like you; and I will put My words
in His mouth, and He will speak to them all that
I command Him.

The first crucial point in Deuteronomy is that Moses as
the spokesman of God was like an aged, loving father speaking to his children with much love and concern. This book
contains God's word more than any other book of the Bible—
the words of God spoken through this one spokesman.

Some may think that there is more of God's word in Job
than in Deuteronomy. This view, however, is not correct. The
book of Job does contain God's word, but it also contains the
word of Job and his three friends, who spoke according to
human opinion, logic, philosophy, and psychology. Eventually, the young man Elihu spoke what was on God's heart. In
the book of Job God's word is not as abundant as in the book
of Deuteronomy.

Moses spoke for God for forty years, from the age of eighty
to the age of one hundred twenty. He was a person not only
soaked and saturated with the thought of God but also constituted with the speaking God Himself. So the word that proceeded out of his mouth was the word of God spoken through
this one spokesman. (*Life-study of Deuteronomy*, p. 14)

Today's Reading

In Deuteronomy 18:15-19 Moses spoke concerning Jehovah God's raising up of a Prophet (the coming Christ) like
Moses for the children of Israel. Acts 3:22 applies these verses
to Christ, indicating that Christ is the Prophet promised by
God to His people, the children of Israel.

The Prophet was to be from among their brothers (Deut.
18:15a). This indicates that Christ as the coming Prophet
would be human as well as divine, that He would be God

incarnated to be a man, the God-man. As God, Christ could not be from among the Jews as a brother, but as the incarnated One, the One who has put on human nature and who was a Jew, Christ was from among His brothers.

Moses told the children of Israel that they were to listen to this Prophet (Deut. 18:15b). (*Life-study of Deuteronomy,* pp. 140-141)

A prophet is God's spokesman, not mainly to predict things that are coming but to speak for God and speak forth God by God's revelation. In his forty years of leading the children of Israel, Moses continually spoke to them for God, and especially in Deuteronomy he repeatedly spoke God's words to them. Although it was Moses who spoke, he did not speak his own words; he spoke God's words. He spoke for God, spoke forth God, and spoke God into the children of Israel. Every word he spoke also became God's word. As such a prophet Moses was also a type of Christ (Acts 3:22-23).

[Deuteronomy 18:15] indicates that Moses' being a prophet was not of his own doing or of his own making; he was raised up by God. So also is Christ as God's Prophet.

Moses was raised up by God as God's prophet [v. 18]. In his forty years of leading the children of Israel, he was God's spokesman, speaking for God to them all that God commanded him. Likewise, when Christ was on the earth, He spoke to His disciples for God; His teaching was not His but was according to what the Father had taught Him (John 7:16; 8:28b). He did not speak from Himself; as the Father said to Him, so He spoke (John 12:49-50). As God's Prophet, He spoke for God, spoke forth God, and revealed God to the disciples. Today He is still in us speaking for God, speaking forth God, and speaking God into us. (*Truth Lessons—Level Three,* vol. 1, pp. 118-119)

Further Reading: Life-study of Deuteronomy, msgs. 2, 20, 28-29; *Truth Lessons—Level Three,* vol. 1, lsn. 13

Enlightenment and inspiration:_____

_____

_____

_____

Morning Nourishment

John **For He whom God has sent speaks the words of**
3:34 **God, for He gives the Spirit not by measure.**
8:28 **...I do nothing from Myself, but as My Father**
      has taught Me, I speak these things.
Rev. **...His name is called the Word of God.**
19:13

[Deuteronomy 18:18] indicates that God would raise up this Prophet through the incarnation of Christ to speak the word of God (John 1:14; 3:34; 7:16-17; Heb. 1:2a). When the Lord Jesus came, He surely spoke God's word. To speak God's word is to dispense God, to speak God forth into others. This is what the Lord Jesus did as the Prophet raised up by God. (*Life-study of Deuteronomy,* p. 141)

Today's Reading

In His earthly ministry the Lord Jesus never spoke His own word. Whatever He spoke was the Father's speaking. On one occasion He said, "My teaching is not Mine, but His who sent Me" (John 7:16). In not speaking from Himself the Lord did not seek His own glory but the glory of the One who sent Him (v. 18). Instead of speaking His own words, He spoke God. When He spoke God's word, God was expressed through His speaking. God came forth from Him through His words. He lived a life of speaking God, a life of expressing God for His glory.

In John 12:49 and 50 the Lord Jesus says, "I have not spoken from Myself; but the Father who sent Me, He Himself has given Me commandment, what to say and what to speak. And I know that His commandment is eternal life. The things therefore that I speak, even as the Father has said to Me, so I speak." This clearly reveals that in His ministry the Lord spoke the Father's word. In particular, the commandment that the Father gave Him to speak was eternal life. Therefore, He came with living words, and whoever receives His words will have eternal life.

In John 14:10 the Lord Jesus goes on to say, "The words

that I say to you I do not speak from Myself, but the Father who abides in Me does His works." Once again the Lord makes it clear that He did not speak His own word but the Father's word. While the Son was speaking in this way, the Father was working. The Son's speaking was the Father's working.

In His ministry the Lord Jesus revealed the Father to the disciples. Matthew 11:27 says, "No one fully knows the Son except the Father; neither does anyone fully know the Father except the Son and him to whom the Son wills to reveal Him." This indicates that to know the Father requires the Son's revelation. The Greek word for *wills* in verse 27 means to deliberately exercise the will through counsel. This the Lord did in revealing the Father to the disciples.

In His prayer to the Father before His crucifixion the Lord Jesus said, "I have manifested Your name to the men whom You gave Me out of the world" (John 17:6). The name referred to here is the name Father. The names "God" and "Jehovah" were adequately revealed to man in the Old Testament, but not the name Father, though it is mentioned in Isaiah 9:6; 63:16; and 64:8. In Old Testament times God's people mainly knew that God was Elohim, that is, God, and Jehovah, that is, the ever-existing One, but they did not know much about the title Father. God is His name for creation, and Jehovah is His name for the relationship between Himself and man. Eventually, the Son came and worked in the Father's name (John 5:43; 10:25) to manifest the Father to the ones whom the Father gave Him and to make the Father's name known to them, the name which reveals the Father as the source of life (5:26) for the propagation and multiplication of life, of whom many sons are born (1:12-13) to express the Father. Hence, the Father's name is very much related to the divine life. (*The Conclusion of the New Testament,* pp. 743-746)

Further Reading: The Conclusion of the New Testament, msgs. 22, 69, 90; *Truth Lessons—Level Three,* vol. 2, lsn. 30

_Enlightenment and inspiration:______
_____
_____
_____

Morning Nourishment

1 Cor. But to the rest I say, I, not the Lord, If any brother
7:12 has an unbelieving wife and she consents to dwell
with him, he must not leave her.

25 Now concerning virgins I have no commandment
of the Lord, but I give *my* opinion as one who has
been shown mercy by the Lord to be faithful.

Every word spoken by Moses in Deuteronomy was God's word. Moses might have expressed something of his own feeling, but even this became the word of God. His speaking in Deuteronomy was like Paul's speaking in 1 Corinthians 7. In that chapter Paul said, "I have no commandment of the Lord, but I give my opinion as one who has been shown mercy by the Lord to be faithful" (v. 25). Later, after expressing his opinion, he said, "I think that I also have the Spirit of God" (v. 40). Eventually, because Paul was a man constituted with God, his opinion became a part of God's word as the divine revelation in the New Testament. In his speaking he was one with God; therefore, what he spoke was God's speaking. (*Life-study of Deuteronomy*, p. 14)

Today's Reading

It is important to see this principle of being absolutely one with the Lord in all circumstances, situations, and conditions. If we are mindful of this principle as we read 1 Corinthians 7, we shall see that Paul is utterly one with the Lord and that in his instructions and answers he spontaneously and unconsciously expresses such an absolute spirit. Because Paul had this kind of spirit, he could answer the Corinthians' questions in a clear and absolute way, in a way that would help them also to become one with God in their situation.

Paul's answers are very different from those given by marriage counselors. The advice given by marriage counselors reveals that they are independent of God and even rebellious against Him. In their instructions, advice, and answers they are altogether apart from God. Paul, on the contrary, was absolutely under God, for God, and one with God.

Another very important point revealed in this chapter is that those who love the Lord, who are for Him, and who are one with Him must be willing to accept any kind of circumstance or situation. For example, if a brother's unbelieving wife desires to remain with him, he should accept this situation. But if she decides to leave, he should also accept this circumstance.

It is very important for us to see that God is always in our circumstances. We may say that the circumstances are actually God coming to us in disguise. Apparently we are in a particular circumstance; actually that circumstance is God coming to us and God with us. In verse 24 Paul says, "Each one, brothers, in what status he was called, in this let him remain with God." Notice the words "with God." They indicate that when we take our circumstances, we take God. Both within the circumstances and behind them, God is present.

Once again we see that Paul had an excellent spirit, a spirit which was submissive, content, and satisfied. Paul did not have any complaints. In his spirit he was very submissive and content with his situation. No matter how he was treated, he did not complain. To him, every situation was of the Lord, and he would not initiate anything to change it. Paul could say, "To me, everything works for good. This is the reason I don't want to change anything. I know that when I take my circumstances, I take my God. In every situation is my God, the One whom I love and the One to whom I belong absolutely." What an excellent spirit is displayed in this attitude!

I appreciate 1 Corinthians 7 not primarily for all the answers it gives, but because this chapter conveys the spirit of a person who loves the Lord, who cares for the Lord's interests on earth, who is absolutely for the Lord and one with the Lord, and who in every respect is obedient, submissive, and satisfied with God and the circumstances arranged by Him. (*Life-study of 1 Corinthians,* pp. 373-375)

Further Reading: Life-study of 1 Corinthians, msg. 43

*Enlightenment and inspiration:*_____

_____

_____

_____

Morning Nourishment

1 Cor. But she is more blessed if she so remains, accord-
7:40 ing to my opinion; but I think that I also have the
      Spirit of God.
6:17 But he who is joined to the Lord is one spirit.

First Corinthians 7 is mysterious and deep. In this chapter Paul never utters the words, "Thus saith the Lord." The
reason Paul does not use such an expression is that the apostles' teaching in the New Testament is altogether based on
the principle of incarnation. According to this principle, God
speaks in man's speaking....When the Lord Jesus spoke to the
Pharisees, it seems that He was an ordinary person from Naza-
reth. There was no indication that He was different, and the
Pharisees regarded Him as a man without learning. But the
Lord Jesus is God incarnate. With Him there is the reality
of incarnation. Thus, while He was speaking, God spoke also.
Actually, His speaking was God's speaking. God spoke with
Him. This means that in the Lord Jesus God and man spoke
together as one. This is the principle of incarnation. (*Life-
study of 1 Corinthians*, p. 378)

Today's Reading

On the day of Pentecost the apostles and disciples also
began to speak according to the principle of incarnation. This
is the reason the writings of Peter, John, and Paul recorded in
the Bible could become God's words. Furthermore, these words
are among the contents of the New Testament. Although Paul
writes in 1 Corinthians 7 that certain things he says are not
the Lord's word or the Lord's commandment, everything spoken by Paul in this chapter has nonetheless become part of
the divine revelation in the New Testament. This is because
Paul was a person absolutely one with God....Because Paul
was one with the Lord, when he spoke, the Lord spoke with
him. Thus, with Paul in 1 Corinthians 7 we have an example
of the principle of incarnation.

I would emphasize the importance of touching Paul's spirit
in 1 Corinthians 7. In his answers to the questions raised by

the Corinthian believers, Paul expresses his spirit. This makes it possible for us to sense his spirit. Paul certainly was absolutely for the Lord and one with Him. Even in expressing his opinion, he had the feeling that he also had the Spirit of God. This is the New Testament teaching, and the way we should follow today. Do not follow the superficial Pentecostal way to copy the Old Testament manner of prophesying. Instead, follow Paul's way to touch the depths of the New Testament mystery. This mystery is that the Lord and we, we and the Lord, have become one spirit. (*Life-study of 1 Corinthians,* pp. 378-379, 383-384)

No spiritual experience is as deep as that revealed in 1 Corinthians 7. Here we have a man who tells us that he does not have the Lord's commandment. Then he proceeds to give his own opinion. After giving his opinion, he tells us, "I think that I also have the Spirit of God" [v. 40]. Here Paul seems to be saying, "I am giving you my word, my opinion, without any commandment from the Lord. But I think that I nevertheless have the Spirit of God."

If we had been able to question Paul concerning this, he might have replied, "Brother, I am now practicing what I wrote about in 6:17. It is certainly right to say that he who is joined to the Lord is one spirit. Now when I say that I think I also have the Spirit of God, I am living the Lord. I live the Lord in this one spirit. Even when I give you my opinion, I still have the Spirit of the Lord, although I do not have the boldness to declare with assurance that I have the Spirit. However, those who are childish and shallow may say with assurance that they have the Spirit of God. Actually, they do not have that kind of assurance. But what I am saying is a description of my living of the Lord." If we see this, we will realize that chapter 7 of 1 Corinthians describes something profound. (*CWWL, 1983,* vol. 2, "The Divine Dispensing of the Divine Trinity," pp. 400-401)

Further Reading: CWWL, 1983, vol. 2, "The Divine Dispensing of the Divine Trinity," ch. 28

Enlightenment and inspiration:_____
_____
_____
_____

Morning Nourishment

1 Cor. But to the married I charge, not I but the Lord,
7:10   A wife must not be separated from *her* husband.

2:13   Which things also we speak, not in words taught
       by human wisdom but in words taught by the
       Spirit, interpreting spiritual things with spiri-
       tual *words.*

The principle in 1 Corinthians 7:10 is the same as that in Galatians 2:20, where Paul says, "It is no longer I who live, but it is Christ who lives in me." In both verses we see the principle of incarnation; two persons living as one person. In 1 Corinthians 7:10 we have two persons, the Lord and Paul, speaking as one....Why does Paul not say in this verse, "But to the married the Lord charges"? Why does he say that he charges, yet not he but the Lord? The answer to these questions is that Paul realized that he was one with the Lord and that what he spoke was the Lord's word. Even when he did not claim to have a word from the Lord, because he was one with the Lord, whatever he said was the Lord's word.

Verse 25 says, "Now concerning virgins I have no commandment of the Lord, but I give my opinion as one who has been shown mercy by the Lord to be faithful." A wife should not be separated from her husband. This, the apostle says, is the Lord's commandment (v. 10). But concerning virgins not marrying, he says he has no commandment of the Lord, but he gives his opinion in the following verses. He dares to do this because he has received mercy of the Lord to be faithful to the Lord's interests, and he is really one with the Lord. His opinion expresses the Lord's desire. This is again based on the New Testament principle of incarnation. (*Life-study of 1 Corinthians,* pp. 380-381)

Today's Reading

Some readers of 1 Corinthians may think that Paul was too strong in giving his opinion when he had no commandment from the Lord. Which one of us would dare to say that we have no commandment of the Lord concerning a certain matter, but that we give our opinion? Yet this is the very thing

Paul does in 7:25. Here we see the highest spirituality, the spirituality of a person who is so one with the Lord that even his opinion expresses the Lord's mind. Paul was absolutely one with the Lord and thoroughly saturated with Him. Because his entire being was permeated with the Lord, even his opinion expressed the mind of the Lord. For this reason, we say that verse 25 expresses the highest spirituality.

All these words indicate the New Testament principle of incarnation, that is, God and man, man and God, becoming one. This differs drastically from the principle of Old Testament prophecy—speaking for God. In the Old Testament, as we have pointed out, the word of Jehovah came unto a prophet (Jer. 1:2; Ezek. 1:3), the prophet being simply the mouthpiece of God. But in the New Testament the Lord becomes one with His apostles and they become one with Him. Both speak together. His word becomes their word, and whatever they utter is His word. Hence, the apostle's charge is the Lord's charge (1 Cor. 7:10). What he says, though not by the Lord, still becomes a part of the divine revelation in the New Testament (v. 12). He is so one with the Lord that even when he gives his own opinion, not the commandment of the Lord (v. 25), he still thinks that he also has the Spirit of God. He does not claim definitely to have the Spirit of God, but he *thinks* that he *also* has the Spirit of God. This is the highest spirituality; it is based on the principle of incarnation.

We need to see the principle of incarnation illustrated here and receive mercy and grace from the Lord to speak in a genuine and frank manner without any pretense. In order to speak like this we need to be saturated with the Spirit. Then what we utter or express will be our thought, our opinion, but it will also be something of the Lord because we are one with Him. (*Life-study of 1 Corinthians*, pp. 381-383)

Further Reading: CWWL, 1985, vol. 5, "Speaking for God," ch. 3; *CWWL, 1985*, vol. 4, "Everyone Speaking the Word of God," chs. 1-2

*Enlightenment and inspiration:*_____
_____
_____
_____

Hymns, #782

1 How mysterious, O Lord,
   That Thy Spirit dwells in mine;
   Oh, how marvelous it is—
   Into one, two spirits twine.

2 By the spirit I can walk,
   Spiritual in spirit be;
   By the spirit I can serve
   And in spirit worship Thee.

3 Through Thy Word and by my prayer
   In the spirit touching Thee,
   Lifted high my spirit is,
   Strengthened shall my spirit be.

4 Make my spirit strong, I pray—
   Others' spirits to revive;
   Lift my spirit high and free—
   Others' spirits then may thrive.

5 Every time I speak, O Lord,
   May my spirit actuate;
   And whatever I may do,
   Let my spirit motivate.

6 Every time my spirit acts,
   Others' spirits opened be;
   Every time my spirit moves,
   Others' lifted unto Thee.

7 Lord, have mercy, from above;
   May Thy Spirit breathe on me.
   Then my spirit will be rich,
   Strengthened and refreshed by Thee.

*Composition for prophecy with main point and sub-points:*_____

_____

_____

_____

_____

_____

_____

_____

_____

_____

_____

_____

_____

_____

_____

_____

_____

_____

_____

_____

_____

_____

_____

_____

_____

_____

_____

_____

_____

_____

_____

_____

_____

_____

_____

_____

Christ—the One Cursed and Hanged on a Tree

Scripture Reading: Deut. 21:22-23; 1 Pet. 2:24; Gal. 3:2, 5, 13-14

Day 1 & Day 2

I. **In Deuteronomy 21:22-23 there is a prophecy that Christ would be the cursed One hanging on a tree; here we have a type of the crucified Christ as the One who was hanged on a tree—1 Pet. 2:24:**
    A. A criminal could be executed by being hanged on a tree; he who was hanged was accursed of God—Deut. 21:22-23.
    B. If in a man there was a sin, a cause worthy of death, and he was put to death and was hanged on a tree, his corpse was not to remain overnight on the tree but had to be buried that day, for he who was hanged on a tree was accursed of God—v. 23.
    C. The Lord Jesus was killed by being crucified, that is, by being hanged on a tree, the cross, and He was buried on the day of His crucifixion—Acts 5:30; 10:39; 13:29; John 19:31.

II. **The origin of the curse is man's sin—Gen. 3:17b; Rom. 5:12:**
    A. God brought in the curse after Adam's sin, saying, "Cursed is the ground because of you"—Gen. 3:17b:
        1. As descendants of Adam, all sinners are under the curse; Adam brought us all under the curse—v. 17b; Rom. 5:12, 17-18.
        2. Ultimately, the curse is death; death, including all other sufferings, is the consummation of the curse—vv. 12, 17; 6:16, 21, 23.
    B. After Adam sinned, the earth brought forth thorns because of the curse, so thorns are a sign of being cursed—Gen. 3:18; Heb. 6:8.

III. **The curse is carried out through the law, for the law administers the curse—Gal. 3:10:**

A. The curse was not altogether official until the law was given; the law now declares that all the descendants of Adam are under the curse—Rom. 5:13.

B. The curse, therefore, is related to the law of God, and it is the demand of the righteousness of God upon sinners—3:19.

C. If we try to keep the law, we will be in the flesh and automatically come under the curse: "As many as are of the works of law are under a curse; for it is written, 'Cursed is everyone who does not continue in all the things written in the book of the law to do them'"—Gal. 3:10.

IV. **"Christ has redeemed us out of the curse of the law, having become a curse on our behalf; because it is written, 'Cursed is everyone hanging on a tree'"—v. 13:**

A. On the cross Christ accomplished the great work of bringing us out from the curse of the law, working to bear our sins and to remove the curse—v. 13; 1 Pet. 2:24.

Day 3

B. Christ Himself "bore up our sins in His body on the tree"—v. 24:

1. The word *tree* in 1 Peter 2:24 is the cross made of wood, a Roman instrument of capital punishment used for the execution of malefactors, as prophesied in Deuteronomy 21:23; elsewhere in the New Testament the cross is called a tree— Acts 5:30; 10:39; 13:29.

2. When Christ was on the cross, God took all our sins and put them on the Lamb of God—Isa. 53:6; John 1:29.

3. Christ died once to bear our sins, and He suffered the judgment for us on the cross—Heb. 9:28; Isa. 53:5, 11.

4. In the death of Christ we have died to sins so that we might live to righteousness—Rom. 6:8, 10-11, 18; 1 Pet. 2:24.

C. When Christ bore our sins, He also took our curse—
    John 1:29; Gal. 3:13:

    1. The crown of thorns indicates this; since thorns
        are a sign of the curse, Christ's wearing a crown
        of thorns indicates that He took our curse on
        the cross—John 19:2, 5.

    2. Because Christ was cursed in our place, the
        demand of the law was fulfilled, and He could
        redeem us out of the curse of the law—Gal. 3:10.

    3. Whereas the law condemns us and makes the
        curse official, Christ through His crucifixion has
        redeemed us out of the curse of the law—v. 13.

    4. The curse that came in through Adam's fall has
        been dealt with by Christ's redemption—v. 13.

D. Not only did Christ redeem us out of the curse; He
    even became a curse on our behalf; this indicates
    that He was absolutely abandoned by God—v. 13;
    Mark 15:33-34:

    1. The Lord Jesus was judged by God for the ac-
        complishment of redemption, and God counted
        Him as our suffering Substitute for sin—Isa.
        53:10a.

    2. Our sin and sins and all negative things were
        dealt with on the cross, and God forsook the
        Slave-Savior because of our sin—Mark 15:33-34:

        a. God forsook Christ on the cross because He
            took the place of sinners, bearing our sins
            and being made sin for us—1 Pet. 3:18; 2:24;
            Isa. 53:6; 2 Cor. 5:21.

        b. In the sight of God, Christ became a great
            sinner, and God judged Him as our Substi-
            tute for our sins—John 3:14; Rom. 8:3.

        c. Christ was our Substitute and was even sin
            in the sight of God; therefore, God judged
            Him and even forsook Him.

    3. Because Christ bore our sins and was made sin
        for us, God, in judging Him as our Substitute,
        forsook Him economically—Mark 15:33-34:

   a. The Lord Jesus was born of the begetting
       Spirit as the divine essence, who never left
       Him essentially—Luke 1:35.
   b. When the Lord Jesus, the God-man, died on
       the cross under God's judgment, He had God
       within Him essentially as His divine being;
       nevertheless, He was forsaken by the right-
       eous and judging God economically—Matt.
       1:18, 20; 27:46:
       1) Because the Lord Jesus was conceived
           of the Holy Spirit and was born of God
           and with God, He had the Holy Spirit as
           the intrinsic essence of His divine being;
           thus, it was not possible for God to for-
           sake Him essentially—1:18, 20.
       2) Christ was forsaken by God economically
           when the Spirit, who had descended upon
           Him as the economical power for the car-
           rying out of His ministry (3:16), left Him;
           however, the essence of God remained in
           His being, and He therefore died on the
           cross as the God-man—1 John 1:7.

Day 4

E. In His humanity as the seed of Abraham, Christ
    was crucified and became a curse on our behalf to
    redeem us out of the curse of the law—Gal. 3:13, 29:
    1. Genesis 22:17-18a and 28:14 are a prophecy that
        Abraham's seed would be a great blessing to
        all mankind, for all nations would be blessed
        through his seed.
    2. Christ, the seed of Abraham, has brought God
        to us and us to God for our enjoyment of God's
        blessing—Gal. 3:8-12, 16.
    3. The promise given to Abraham was that God
        Himself would come to be the seed of Abraham,
        and this seed would be a blessing to all the
        nations by becoming the all-inclusive Spirit for
        mankind to receive—v. 14; 1 Cor. 15:45b.

V. As the seed of Abraham, Christ was made a curse for us "in order that the blessing of Abraham might come to the Gentiles in Christ Jesus, that we might receive the promise of the Spirit through faith"—Gal. 3:14:

   A. The blessing of Abraham is the blessing promised by God to him for all the nations of the earth—Gen. 12:3.

   B. This promise was fulfilled and this blessing has come to the nations in Christ through His redemption by the cross—Gal. 3:1, 13-14.

   C. The context of Galatians 3:14 indicates that the Spirit is the blessing that God promised to Abraham for all the nations and that has been received by the believers through faith in Christ—vv. 2, 5:

      1. The physical aspect of the blessing that God promised to Abraham was the good land, which was a type of the all-inclusive Christ—Gen. 12:7; 13:15; 17:8; 26:3-4; Col. 1:12.

      2. The Spirit is the compound Spirit, who is God Himself processed in His Trinity through incarnation, crucifixion, resurrection, ascension, and descension for us to receive as our life and our everything—Phil. 1:19.

      3. Since Christ is realized as the all-inclusive life-giving Spirit (1 Cor. 15:45; 2 Cor. 3:17), the blessing of the promised Spirit equals the blessing of the good land; actually, the Spirit as the realization of Christ in our experience is the good land.

      4. Our spiritual blessing for eternity will be to inherit the Spirit, the consummation of the processed Triune God as our inheritance—Gal. 3:14.

      5. In the new heaven and the new earth in the New Jerusalem, we will enjoy the processed Triune God, who is the all-inclusive, consummated, life-giving Spirit—Rev. 22:1; John 7:37-39.

      6. Today our Christian life is a life of receiving the Spirit through faith—Gal. 3:2, 5, 14.

Morning Nourishment

Deut. And if in a man there is a sin, a cause *worthy* of
21:22- death, and he is put to death, and you hang him
23 on a tree; his corpse shall not remain overnight
on the tree, but you must bury him on that day.
For he who is hanged is accursed of God...

Acts The God of our fathers has raised Jesus, whom
5:30 you slew by hanging *Him* on a tree.

Deuteronomy 21:22-23 is concerned with the hanging of
a criminal on a tree. A criminal could be executed not only by
being stoned but also by being hanged on a tree. Whereas
Stephen was killed by being stoned (Acts 7:58-59), the Lord
Jesus was killed by being crucified, that is, by being hanged
on a tree. The one hanged on a tree in Deuteronomy 21:22-23
is therefore a type of the crucified Christ.

If in a man there was a sin, a cause worthy of death, and he
was put to death and was hanged on a tree, his corpse was not
to remain overnight on the tree but had to be buried on that
day, for he who was hanged was accursed of God (vv. 22-23).
This was exactly the situation when the Lord Jesus was crucified (John 19:31). He was buried on the day of His crucifixion.

The one who was cursed and hanged on the tree was a type
of Christ, who was cursed and hanged on the cross to redeem
us out of the curse of the law (Gal. 3:13). (*Life-study of Deuteronomy,* p. 126)

Today's Reading

Deuteronomy 21:22-23 is an illustration of an important
principle—that the Old Testament was written not mainly
for the sake of the children of Israel but mainly for the sake
of Christ. The primary purpose of the Old Testament is to
portray Christ in various ways. This is the reason that Luke
24:27 says of the Lord Jesus, "Beginning from Moses and
from all the prophets, He explained to them clearly in all the
Scriptures the things concerning Himself." Furthermore, in

opening the minds of His disciples to understand the Scriptures, He said to them, "All the things written in the Law of Moses and the Prophets and Psalms concerning Me must be fulfilled" (Luke 24:44). In Deuteronomy 21 we have a type of Christ as the One who was hanged on the tree, on the cross. Peter used the word *tree* when speaking of the Lord's crucifixion: "Who Himself bore up our sins in His body on the tree" (1 Pet. 2:24). (*Life-study of Deuteronomy*, pp. 126-127)

As the seed of Abraham, Christ in His humanity was crucified and became a curse on our behalf to redeem us out of the curse of the law. Galatians 3:1 mentions that Jesus Christ was crucified. Verse 13 goes on to say, "Christ has redeemed us out of the curse of the law, having become a curse on our behalf; because it is written, 'Cursed is everyone hanging on a tree.'" Christ as our Substitute on the cross not only bore the curse for us but also became a curse for us. The curse of the law issued from the sin of man (Gen. 3:17). When Christ took away our sin on the cross, He redeemed us out of the curse of the law.

Through his fall, Adam brought us all under the curse; as fallen descendants of Adam, we the sinners were under the curse. The origin of the curse is man's sin. God brought in the curse after Adam's sin, saying, "Cursed is the ground because of you" (v. 17). The sign of the curse is thorns (v. 18). For this reason, after Adam's sin, the earth brought forth thorns.

However, the curse was not altogether official until the law was given. The law now declares that all the fallen descendants of Adam are under the curse. In other words, the curse is carried out through the law. This means that the law administers the curse. Therefore, the curse is related to the law of God; it is the demand of the righteous God upon sinners. (*The Conclusion of the New Testament*, pp. 3286-3287)

Further Reading: Life-study of Deuteronomy, msg. 18; Truth Lessons—Level Three, vol. 2, lsn. 32

Enlightenment and inspiration:_____

_____

_____

_____

Morning Nourishment

Rom. **For if, by the offense of the one, death reigned**
5:17 **through the one, much more those who receive**
the abundance of grace and of the gift of right-
eousness will reign in life through the One, Jesus
Christ.
6:23 **For the wages of sin is death, but the gift of God**
is eternal life in Christ Jesus our Lord.

Whereas the law condemns us and makes the curse official, Christ through His crucifixion has redeemed us out of
the curse of the law. On the cross He was even made a curse
for us. Therefore, the curse that came in through Adam's fall
has been dealt with by Christ's redemption.

When Christ bore our sins, He also took our curse. The
crown of thorns indicates this (John 19:2, 5). Since thorns are
a sign of the curse, Christ's wearing a crown of thorns indicates that He took our curse on the cross. Because Christ was
cursed in our place, the demand of the law was fulfilled, and
He could redeem us from the curse of the law. (*The Conclusion
of the New Testament,* p. 3287)

Today's Reading

Not only did Christ redeem us out from the curse; He even
became a curse on our behalf. This indicates that He was absolutely abandoned by God. God forsook Christ economically
and also considered Him a curse. On the cross Christ accomplished the great work of bringing us out from the curse of the
law, working to bear our sins and to remove the curse.

In His creation of man, God intended that man might enjoy
God as his blessing. But through the fall of Adam, man lost God
as his blessing and enjoyment. Not only so, since man did not
know that he was totally fallen, incurable, and hopeless, he
tried to please God by his own effort. This forced God to decree
the law in order to expose man's fallen condition. Knowing that
man could not keep the law, God gave man the law, not for
him to keep it but for man to realize that he is utterly fallen
and hopeless.

Here we need to see that before decreeing the law, God promised Abraham a blessing: Out of him would come a seed who would be a blessing not only to his own house, his race, but also to all the nations, all the Gentiles. With Adam we have sin and the curse, but with Abraham we have God's promise. The background of this promise was the curse upon mankind. Because mankind was under a curse, man's direction was downward. But God came in, called Abraham, and promised that in his seed, all the nations—mankind under a curse—would be blessed.

Yet the children of Israel did not realize that God's intention was not for them to try to keep the law but to bring them back to the promise given to their forefather, Abraham, through the law. Because the children of Israel did not see that the function of the law was to expose their fallen condition and to restore them to the promised blessing, they tried to keep the law, thereby coming under the curse of the law (Deut. 27:15-26).

Through His incarnation Christ came as the seed of Abraham, and through His crucifixion Christ died on the cross to be a curse on our behalf. In doing so, Christ removed the curse from all those who believe in Him. Through His work on the cross, Christ became a curse on our behalf and redeemed us out of the curse of the law so that the blessing God promised to Abraham would be bestowed on all those who believe in Christ.

If we try to keep the law, we will be in the flesh and automatically come under the curse, for those who are of the works of the law are under the curse [cf. Gal. 3:10]. Instead of trying to keep the law, we should thank the law for exposing us and then bid it farewell. We should leave the law and go to Christ and to the cross. (*The Conclusion of the New Testament,* pp. 3287-3288)

Further Reading: The Conclusion of the New Testament, msgs. 15, 17, 37, 71, 80, 125, 127, 327, 384; *CWWL, 1994-1997,* vol. 5, "Crystallization-study of the Humanity of Christ," ch. 1

Enlightenment and inspiration:_____
_____
_____
_____

Morning Nourishment

1 Pet.
2:24 Who Himself bore up our sins in His body on the tree, in order that we, having died to sins, might live to righteousness; by whose bruise you were healed.

Mark
15:34 And at the ninth hour Jesus cried with a loud voice, Eloi, Eloi, lama sabachthani? which is interpreted, My God, My God, why have You forsaken Me?

When God was judging Christ as our Substitute made sin for us and bearing our sins, God forsook Christ economically....The sixth hour [in Matthew 27:45] is our twelve o'clock noon, and the ninth [in verse 46] is our three o'clock in the afternoon. The Lord Jesus was crucified at the third hour, at our nine o'clock in the morning (Mark 15:25), and He suffered on the cross for six hours. In the first three hours He was persecuted by men for doing God's will; in the last three hours He was judged by God for the accomplishment of our redemption. During that time God counted Him as our suffering Substitute for sin (Isa. 53:10). Hence, darkness came over all the land because our sin and sins and all negative things were dealt with there, and God forsook Him because of our sin. God forsook Christ on the cross because He took the place of sinners (1 Pet. 3:18), bearing our sins (1 Pet. 2:24; Isa. 53:6) and being made sin for us (2 Cor. 5:21). (*The Conclusion of the New Testament*, pp. 176-177)

Today's Reading

According to the four Gospels, the Lord Jesus was on the cross for six hours. During the first three hours, men did many unrighteous things to Him. They persecuted and mocked Him. Thus, in the first three hours the Lord suffered man's unrighteous treatment. But at the sixth hour, twelve noon, God came in, and there was darkness over all the land until the ninth hour, until three o'clock in the afternoon. The coming of darkness was God's doing, and in the midst of it the Lord cried out the words quoted in Matthew 27:46. When the

Lord was suffering the persecution of man, God was with Him, and He enjoyed the presence of God. But at the end of the first three hours, God forsook Him, and darkness came. Unable to tolerate this, the Lord shouted loudly, "My God, My God, why have You forsaken Me?" As we have pointed out, God forsook Him because He was our Substitute bearing our sins. Isaiah 53 reveals that this was the time God put our sins on Him. In the three hours from twelve noon to three o'clock in the afternoon, the righteous God put all our sins upon this Substitute and judged Him righteously for our sins. God forsook Him because during these hours He was a sinner there on the cross; He was even made sin. On the one hand, the Lord bore our sins; on the other hand, He was made sin for us. Therefore, according to His righteousness, God judged Him and forsook Him economically.

The Lord was born of the begetting Spirit, who is God reaching man, as the divine essence, who never left Him essentially. Even when He was on the cross crying out, "My God, My God, why have You forsaken Me?" He still had the begetting Spirit (God in the essential sense) as the divine essence. Then who left Him? It was the anointing Spirit (God in the economical sense), through whom He presented Himself as the God-man to be the all-inclusive sacrifice to God (Heb. 9:14), who left Him economically. After God accepted Christ as the all-inclusive offering, the anointing Spirit left Him. But although the anointing Spirit left Him economically, the Lord still had the begetting Spirit essentially.

When the Lord Jesus, the God-man, died on the cross under God's judgment, He had God within Him essentially as His divine being. Nevertheless, He was forsaken by the righteous and judging God economically. (*The Conclusion of the New Testament,* pp. 177-178)

Further Reading: CWWL, 1985, vol. 3, "Elders' Training, Book 6: The Crucial Points of the Truth in Paul's Epistles," ch. 5

*Enlightenment and inspiration:*_____
_____
_____
_____

Morning Nourishment

Gal. Christ has redeemed us out of the curse of the
3:13 law, having become a curse on our behalf; because it is written, "Cursed is everyone hanging
on a tree."
29 And if you are of Christ, then you are Abraham's
seed, heirs according to promise.

In Galatians 3:1-22 Christ is unveiled as the seed of
Abraham. According to Genesis 22:17-18a the Lord promised
Abraham, "I will surely bless you and will greatly multiply
your seed....And in your seed all the nations of the earth
shall be blessed." In this prophecy we have the promise that
Abraham's seed would be a great blessing to all mankind,
for all nations would be blessed through his seed.

This prophecy was repeated to Isaac in Genesis 26:4 and
again to Jacob in Genesis 28:14. These three verses are not
three prophecies but one prophecy of Christ as the seed of Abraham. The fulfillment of this prophetic word is not only in Matthew 1:1, which says that Christ is the son of Abraham, but
also in Galatians 3:16, which says, "To Abraham were the promises spoken and to his seed. He does not say, And to the seeds,
as concerning many, but as concerning one: 'And to your seed,'
who is Christ." Christ was born as a descendant of Abraham,
born of the chosen race. Therefore, He was the seed of Abraham. (*The Conclusion of the New Testament*, p. 3285)

Today's Reading

As the seed of Abraham, Christ in His humanity blesses all
the nations with the gospel of Christ (Gal. 3:8-12, 16). He has
brought God to us and us to God for our enjoyment of God's
blessing. He brings blessings to the nations. Whether Jews or
Gentiles, all will be blessed in Him (Gen. 22:18a)....Galatians
3:14 indicates that the blessing is the Spirit as the consummation of the Triune God. When we receive the Spirit, we receive the Triune God as eternal life to be our blessing. Through
faith in Christ, we have received the Spirit. The Spirit is also
called the Spirit of grace (Heb. 10:29). When the blessing that

God gave to Abraham comes to us, it is grace; this grace is the seed of Abraham. Since Christ is now the Spirit (2 Cor. 3:17), He is not only the seed who inherits the promises but also the blessing of the promises to be inherited by us.

According to Galatians 3:16, Christ is the seed of Abraham, the Heir who inherits the promises. Here Christ is the unique seed who inherits the promises. Hence, in order to inherit the promised blessing, we must be one with Christ. Outside of Him we cannot inherit the promises given by God to Abraham. In God's eyes Abraham has only one seed, Christ. We must be in Him that we may participate in the promises given to Abraham.

According to Galatians 3:14, the promise given to Abraham was that God Himself would come to be the seed of Abraham, and this seed would be a blessing to all the nations by becoming the all-inclusive Spirit for mankind to receive (1 Cor. 15:45b). God's blessing of Abraham eventually issued in Christ as the unique seed in whom all the nations of the earth are blessed (Acts 3:25-26; Gal. 3:16). All the believers in Christ, as members of the corporate Christ (1 Cor. 12:12), are included in this seed as the heirs of God's promised blessing (Gal. 3:7, 29).

The blessing of the gospel promised to Abraham is the all-inclusive Spirit, the Spirit compounded with Christ's divinity, His humanity, His human living, His all-inclusive death with its effectiveness, His powerful resurrection with its life power, and His ascension. This compound Spirit is the Spirit spoken of in John 7:39....The Holy Spirit was there, but the all-inclusive, compound Spirit was not yet, because by that time, when Jesus spoke those words, He had not yet been glorified; that is, He had not yet been crucified and resurrected (Luke 24:26). It was through His crucifixion and resurrection that Christ became a life-giving Spirit, the compound Spirit, who is the consummation of the processed Triune God. (*The Conclusion of the New Testament,* pp. 3285-3286, 3290-3291)

Further Reading: Life-study of Galatians, msgs. 12-13, 15; *Truth Lessons—Level Four,* vol. 1, lsn. 2

_Enlightenment and inspiration:______
_____
_____
_____

Morning Nourishment

Gen. And I will bless those who bless you...; and in
12:3 you all the families of the earth will be blessed.

Col. Giving thanks to the Father, who has qualified
1:12 you for a share of the allotted portion of the
saints in the light.

2 Cor. And the Lord is the Spirit; and where the Spirit
3:17 of the Lord is, there is freedom.

Christ as the seed of Abraham was crucified and became
a curse on our behalf to redeem us out of the curse of the law
in order that we might receive the Spirit as the blessing of the
gospel promised to Abraham, the promise that all the nations
would be blessed in Him. Galatians 3:14 says, "In order that
the blessing of Abraham might come to the Gentiles in Christ
Jesus, that we might receive the promise of the Spirit through
faith." This verse combines the promise of the Spirit with the
blessing of Abraham. The blessing of Abraham is the blessing
promised by God to Abraham (Gen. 12:3) for all the nations of
the earth. This promise was fulfilled and this blessing has come
to the nations in Christ through His redemption by the cross.
The context of Galatians 3:14 indicates that the Spirit is the
blessing which God promised to Abraham for all the nations
and which has been received by the believers through faith in
Christ. (*The Conclusion of the New Testament,* p. 3289)

Today's Reading

The Spirit is the compound Spirit, who is God Himself
processed in His Trinity through incarnation, crucifixion, resurrection, ascension, and descension for us to receive as our
life and our everything. This is the focus of the gospel of God.
The physical aspect of the blessing that God promised to Abraham was the good land (Gen. 12:7; 13:15; 17:8; 26:3-4), which
was a type of the all-inclusive Christ (Col. 1:12). Since Christ
is eventually realized as the all-inclusive life-giving Spirit
(1 Cor. 15:45b; 2 Cor. 3:17), the blessing of the promised Spirit
corresponds to the blessing of the promised land. Actually, the

Spirit as the realization of Christ in our experience is the good
land as the source of God's bountiful supply for us to enjoy.

Our blessing is God Himself, who is embodied in Christ
and realized as the Spirit to be dispensed into us for our enjoyment. In the universe only God Himself is a blessing; all else
is vanity of vanities (Eccl. 1:2). Even the entire universe cannot compare with our Triune God. If we have God, we have
the blessing. However, God becoming our blessing involved
a process. Just as food must be cooked to become our blessing, God had to be "cooked" in order to be our blessing. Before
passing through a process, God was a "raw" God. By passing
through a process, God became the "cooked" God to be our
life and life supply. This God in His totality is the processed,
consummated, all-inclusive, life-giving, indwelling Spirit. He
as the wonderful Spirit is the blessing from God to us. The
blessing of the gospel is the Spirit, the sum total and the aggregate of the processed Triune God.

Our spiritual blessing for eternity is to inherit the Spirit,
the consummation of the processed Triune God, as our inheri-
tance. In the new heaven and new earth in the New Jerusalem,
we will enjoy the processed Triune God, who is the all-inclusive,
consummated, life-giving Spirit (Rev. 22:1; John 7:37-39). Even
today, the most enjoyable thing to us is the indwelling Spirit.

In the full gospel of God, in Christ we have received not
only the blessing of forgiveness, washing, and cleansing; even
more, we have received the greatest blessing, the Triune God—
the Father, Son, and Spirit—as the processed, all-inclusive
life-giving Spirit dwelling in us in a most subjective way for
our enjoyment. Oh, what a blessing that we can enjoy such an
all-inclusive One as our daily portion! (*The Conclusion of the
New Testament,* pp. 3289-3290)

Further Reading: CWWL, 1984, vol. 3, "God's New Testament
    Economy," ch. 14; *CWWL, 1972,* vol. 3, "Enjoying Christ
    as the All-inclusive Spirit for the Practical, Genuine, and
    Real Church Life," ch. 5

Enlightenment and inspiration:_____
_____
_____
_____

Summary of our Xtain LIFE

Morning Nourishment

Gal. This only I wish to learn from you, Did you re-
3:2 ceive the Spirit out of the works of law or out of
the hearing of faith?

5 He therefore who bountifully supplies to you the
Spirit and does works of power among you, *does
He do it* out of the works of law or out of the
hearing of faith?

The Spirit is the consummation of the Triune God having gone through many processes in Christ. This life-giving Spirit is the blessing of the gospel. The blessing of the gospel is the processed Triune God reaching us as the Spirit. In this compound, all-inclusive Spirit are all of Christ's person and process, including His divinity, humanity, crucifixion for Him to accomplish redemption, resurrection for Him to give life to us, and ascension for Him to be the Lord of all (Rom. 8:11; 2 Cor. 3:18)....The Spirit is everything to us to live the Christian life....If we have the Spirit, we have God, man, redemption, and forgiveness of sins. The Spirit is our God, our Father, our Lord, our Redeemer, our Savior, and our Shepherd; the Spirit is our life, our life supply, our righteousness, our sanctification, our transformation, and our redemption. The all-inclusive Spirit is the processed and consummated Triune God given to us as the blessing. We should praise the Lord that we have received the Spirit as such a blessing and may enjoy Him all the time through eternity. (*The Conclusion of the New Testament,* pp. 3293-3294) AMEN

AMEN

Today's Reading

Galatians reveals the way to receive, experience, and enjoy the all-inclusive Christ as the all-inclusive life-giving Spirit—the aggregate of the all-embracing blessing of the full gospel of God: by God's revealing of Christ in us (1:16a; Eph. 1:17; Gen. 13:14-18; Eph. 3:8, 19); by our receiving of Christ out of the hearing of faith (Gal. 3:2); by being born according to the Spirit and by being given the Spirit of God's Son into our hearts (4:29b, 6); by putting on Christ through the baptism that puts us into Christ (3:27); by being identified with Him in His death so that it may be no longer we who live but He who lives in us (2:20); by living and walking by the Spirit (5:16, 25); by having Christ formed in us through travail (4:19); by sowing unto the Spirit with the desire and aim of the Spirit in view, to accomplish what the Spirit desires (6:7-8); by boasting in the cross of Christ and living a new creation (vv. 14-15); and by enjoying the grace of the Lord Jesus Christ with our spirit (vv. 17-18).

Through Adam's fall the human race was brought under the curse, but God promised Abraham that in his seed the nations...would be blessed. Christ has fulfilled God's promise to Abraham....Christ as the seed of Abraham has redeemed us out of the curse of the law so that the blessing of Abraham might come to the nations in Him. Christ died a substitutionary death on the cross to deliver us from the curse brought in by Adam. Then in resurrection Christ, who was the unique seed of Abraham as the last Adam, became the life-giving Spirit. The resurrected Christ as the life-giving Spirit is the transfigured descendant of Abraham, the seed of Abraham, dispensed into us to make us the sons of Abraham, the corporate seed of Abraham, those who can receive and inherit the consummated Spirit as the blessing of Abraham (3:7, 14; 4:28)....Before we believed into Christ and were saved, we were cursed under the law....As the seed of Abraham, Christ brought to us the processed and consummated Triune God as our blessing for our enjoyment. The all-inclusive Spirit, who the all-inclusive Christ as the seed of Abraham has become, is the aggregate of the all-embracing blessing of the full gospel of God in Christ for the divine dispensing according to the divine economy. (*The Conclusion of the New Testament,* pp. 3294-3295)

Further Reading: CWWL, 1965, vol. 3, "The Spirit in the Epistles," ch. 5; *CWWL, 1965,* vol. 3, "Christ as the Spirit in the Epistles," ch. 4; *CWWL, 1966,* vol. 2, "The Divine Spirit with the Human Spirit in the Epistles," ch. 6

*Enlightenment and inspiration:*_____

_____

_____

_____

Hymns, #539

1 O Lord, Thou art in me as life
      And everything to me!
    Subjective and available,
      Thus I experience Thee.

      O Lord, Thou art the Spirit!
        How dear and near to me!
      How I admire Thy marvelous
        Availability!

2 To all my needs, both great and small,
      Thou art the rich supply;
    So ready and sufficient too
      For me now to apply.

3 Thy sweet anointing with Thy might
      In weakness doth sustain;
    By Thy supply of energy
      My strength Thou dost maintain.

4 Thy law of life in heart and mind
      My conduct regulates;
    The wealth of Thy reality
      My being saturates.

5 Oh, Thou art ever one with me,
      Unrivaled unity!
    One spirit with me all the time
      For all eternity!

*Composition for prophecy with main point and sub-points:*_____

_____
_____
_____
_____
_____
_____
_____
_____
_____
_____
_____
_____
_____
_____
_____
_____
_____
_____
_____
_____
_____
_____
_____
_____
_____
_____
_____
_____
_____
_____
_____
_____
_____
_____
_____

Enjoying Christ with God
on the Ground of Oneness

Scripture Reading: Deut. 12:5, 8, 11, 13-14, 17-18, 21, 26-27; Psa.
48:2, 11-12; 80:17-19

Day 1

I. **Deuteronomy 12 reveals the enjoyment of Christ
with God at the unique place of God's choice for
the keeping of the oneness of God's people—
vv. 5-8, 11-14, 17-18, 21, 26-27; 14:22-23; 16:16; cf.
1 Cor. 10:6, 11; Rom. 15:4:**

A. The children of Israel were not allowed to worship
God and enjoy the offerings they presented to God
in the place of their choice (Deut. 12:8, 13, 17); they
were to worship God in the place of His choice, the
place where His name, His habitation, and His
altar were (vv. 5-6), by bringing their tithes, offerings, and sacrifices to Him there (vv. 5, 11, 14, 18,
21, 26-27; 14:22-23; 15:19-20; 16:16).

B. The place of God's unique choice for His worship in
Deuteronomy 12 signifies our meeting on the ground
of locality for the expression of the one Body in practicality (signified by Jerusalem) and for the reality
of the one Body in actuality (signified by Zion within
Jerusalem)—Psa. 48:2; 50:2; Rev. 1:11; 2:7.

C. The revelation in the New Testament concerning
the worship of God corresponds to the revelation
in Deuteronomy 12 in the following ways:

1. The people of God should always be one; there
should be no divisions among them—Psa. 133;
John 17:11, 21-23; 1 Cor. 1:10; Eph. 4:3.

2. The unique name into which God's people should
gather is the name of the Lord Jesus Christ, the
reality of which name is the Spirit; to be desig-
nated by any other name is to be denominated,
divided; this is spiritual fornication—Matt. 18:20;
1 Cor. 1:12; 12:3; Rev. 3:8.

3. In the New Testament God's habitation, His dwelling place, is particularly located in our mingled spirit, our human spirit regenerated and indwelt by the divine Spirit; in our meeting for the worship of God, we must exercise our spirit and do everything in our spirit—Eph. 2:22; John 4:21-24; 1 Cor. 14:15.

4. In our worship of God we must have the genuine application of the cross of Christ, signified by the altar, by rejecting the flesh, the self, and the natural life and worshipping God with Christ and Christ alone—Psa. 43:4a; Matt. 16:24; Gal. 2:20.

5. The place that God has chosen for His worship is a place full of the enjoyment of the riches of Christ and a place full of rejoicing—Deut. 12:7, 12, 18; 14:23; Eph. 3:8; Phil. 4:4; 1 Cor. 14:3, 4b, 26, 31.

D. Wherever we may be, we should be gathered into the Lord's name, in our spirit, and with the cross; if we all do this, we all will meet in the same place, although we meet in different localities; this one place is the ground of the unique oneness—Deut. 12:5-6; Jer. 32:39:

Day 2

1. Apparently, we are divided by geography, for we meet in separate cities all over the world on the scriptural ground of locality—the practice of having one church for one city, one city with only one church—Acts 8:1; 13:1; Rev. 1:11.

2. Actually, in spite of geographical separation, we all meet in the same place—in the name of the Lord Jesus, in our mingled spirit, and with the cross; this is the oneness, and this is the ground for the proper worship of God:

    a. Many Christians are divided by their preferences; in the Lord's recovery we must not be for our preference but for the Lord's pres-

ence as the Spirit of reality, the reality of His
name—Matt. 18:20; 1 Cor. 1:10; Exo. 33:14.

b. The fulfillment of the type in Deuteronomy 12 is not a matter of a geographical place
but a matter of our spirit—John 4:21-24.

c. At the entrance of the church there is the
cross, and in order to meet as the church, we
must experience the cross for the crucifying
of the self, for the overthrowing of "reasonings and every high thing rising up against
the knowledge of God" (2 Cor. 10:5), and for
the exalting of Christ alone so that He may
be all and in all for God's expression and the
unique testimony of oneness—Matt. 16:24;
1 Cor. 2:2; 2 Cor. 10:3-5; Col. 1:10, 18b; 3:10-11.

Day 3

II. **The unique ground of Jerusalem, the place where
the temple as God's dwelling place was built on
Mount Zion, typifies the unique ground of God's
choice, the ground of oneness—Deut. 12:5; 2 Chron.
6:5-6; Ezra 1:2-3:**

A. In the ancient time all the Israelites came together
three times a year at Jerusalem; it was by this unique
place of worship to God, Jerusalem, that the oneness of His people was kept for generations—Deut.
12:5; 16:16.

B. In the New Testament the proper ground of oneness ordained by God is the unique ground of one
church for one locality—Rev. 1:11:

1. The church is constituted of the universal God,
but it exists on earth in many localities; in nature the church is universal in God, but in practice the church is local in a definite place, such as
"the church of God which is in Corinth"—1 Cor.
1:2:

a. *The church of God* means that the church is
not only possessed by God but has God as its

               nature and essence, which are divine, general, universal, and eternal—v. 2a.

    b. *The church...which is in Corinth* refers to a church in a city, remaining in a definite locality and taking it as its standing, ground, and jurisdiction for its administration in business affairs, which is physical, particular, local, and temporal in time—v. 2b.

  2. Without the universal aspect, the church is void of content; without the local aspect, it is impossible for the church to have any expression and practice; the record concerning the establishment of the church in its locality is consistent throughout the New Testament—Acts 8:1; 13:1; 14:23; Rom. 16:1; 1 Cor. 1:2; 2 Cor. 8:1; Gal. 1:2; Rev. 1:4, 11.

Day 4

III. The church life on the ground of oneness is today's Jerusalem; within the church life there must be a group of overcomers, and these overcomers are today's Zion—Psa. 48:2, 11-12:

  A. As the highlight and beauty of the holy city Jerusalem, Zion typifies the overcomers as the high peak, the center, the uplifting, the strengthening, the enriching, the beauty, and the reality of the church—20:2; 53:6a; 87:2.

  B. The overcomers as Zion are the reality of the Body of Christ and consummate the building up of the Body in the local churches to bring in the consummated holy city, New Jerusalem, the Holy of Holies as God's dwelling place, in eternity—Rev. 21:1-3, 16, 22.

  C. The church life is the right place for us to be an overcomer, but this does not mean that as long as we are in the church life, we are an overcomer; it is one thing to be in the church life, but it is another thing to be an overcomer—2:7, 11, 17, 26-28; 3:5, 12, 20-21.

Day 5

IV. **In order to be today's overcomers, we must enjoy Christ with God on the ground of oneness for the exhibition of Christ, the building of the church, and the preparation of Christ's bride—Matt. 16:18; Rev. 19:7:**

A. The children of Israel could enjoy the rich produce of the good land in two ways:

1. The common, private way was to enjoy it as a common portion at any time, in any place, and with anyone—Deut. 12:15.

2. The special, corporate way was to enjoy the top portion, the firstfruits and the firstlings, with all the Israelites at the appointed feasts and in the unique place chosen by God—vv. 5, 8, 11, 13-14, 17-18, 21, 26-27; 14:22-23; 15:19-20; 16:16-17.

B. Likewise, the enjoyment of Christ by His believers is of two aspects:

1. The common, private aspect is to enjoy Christ as our God-allotted portion at every time and in every place—Col. 1:12; 1 Cor. 1:2, 9; Eph. 6:18; 1 Thes. 5:16-18; Rom. 10:12-13.

2. The special, corporate aspect is to enjoy the top portion of Christ in the meetings of the proper church life on the unique ground of oneness, the place chosen by God—1 Cor. 14:3, 4b, 26, 31.

C. We need to live a life of laboring upon Christ, a life of enjoying Christ personally so that we may enjoy Him together collectively for the building up of the Body of Christ as the house of God for God's expression and as the kingdom of God for God's dominion—3:16; 1 Tim. 3:15; Rom. 14:17-18:

1. God's will is for us to enjoy Christ; we must seek to enjoy Christ and experience Him in every situation—Heb. 10:5-10; Phil. 3:7-14; 4:5-8.

2. Christ is rich beyond measure, but the church today is groveling in poverty because the Lord's

children are indolent—Prov. 6:6-11; 24:30-34; 26:14; Matt. 25:26, 30; cf. 1 Cor. 15:58.

3. We must labor on Christ, our good land, so that we may reap some produce of His riches to bring to the church meeting and offer; thus, the meeting will be an exhibition of Christ in His riches and will be a mutual enjoyment of Christ shared by all the attendants before God and with God for the building up of the saints and the church— Col. 2:6-7; 1 Cor. 1:9; 14:3, 31.

4. Whenever we come to the meetings to worship the Lord, we should not come with our hands empty; we must come with our hands full of the produce of Christ—v. 26; Deut. 16:15-17.

5. We meet together to have an exhibition of the Christ upon whom we have labored, the Christ whom we have experienced and enjoyed— 14:22-23.

Day 6

V. **In order to be today's overcomers, we must maintain the ground of oneness, God's unique choice, without elevating anything other than Christ; in the Lord's recovery we elevate Christ and Christ alone—Col. 1:18b; Rev. 2:4; 2 Cor. 4:5; 10:5:**

A. Before the children of Israel could have the full enjoyment of the riches of the good land, they had to utterly destroy the heathen places of worship, the idols, and the names of the idols "on the high mountains and on the hills and under every flourishing tree" (Deut. 12:2); the high mountains and hills signify the exaltation of something other than Christ, and the flourishing trees signify things that are beautiful and attractive—vv. 1-3, 5; 1 Kings 11:7-8; 12:26-31; Num. 33:52.

B. The intrinsic reason for the desolation and degradation of God's people is that Christ is not exalted by them; they do not give Him the preeminence,

the first place, in everything—Psa. 80:1, 3, 7, 15-19;
74:1.

C. The way to be restored from desolation is to exalt
Christ; the enjoyment of Christ with God on the
ground of oneness can be maintained and preserved only when Christ is properly appreciated
and exalted by God's people.

Morning Nourishment

Deut. **But to the place which Jehovah your God will**
12:5-7 **choose out of all your tribes to put His name, to**
His habitation, shall you seek, and there shall you
go. And there you shall bring your burnt offer-
ings and your sacrifices,…and there you shall
eat before Jehovah your God, and you and your
households shall rejoice in all your undertakings,
in which Jehovah your God has blessed you.

The children of Israel were to seek Jehovah and come
unto the place which Jehovah their God would choose out of
all their tribes to put His name, even unto His habitation
with His altar (Deut. 12:5-6). Here we have three things: the
place, the name, and the altar….To fulfill [the] requirements
[of Deuteronomy 12] was to have a center of worship, as Jerusalem would be later, for the keeping of the oneness among
God's people, avoiding the division caused by man's preferences. (*Life-study of Deuteronomy,* pp. 72-73)

Today's Reading

Chapter 12 of Deuteronomy corresponds in at least four
ways to the revelation in the New Testament.

First,…the people of God should always be one….If each
tribe had had its own center for the worship of God, there would
have been twelve divisions among God's people, for each center would have been the ground and the base of a division.
In His wisdom, God…required them to take His choice and
to come three times a year to the unique worship center, even
though travel to that place was inconvenient for many of them.

The principle is the same in the New Testament….God's
children, the believers in Christ, must be one and have the
same center for the worship of God. However,…today…there
are many worship centers, and this has led to divisions.

The divisions among God's people are the result of having
different preferences….The Lord's recovery is a matter of coming back to God's way according to God's preference.

Second,…God's way to keep the oneness of His people is to

have a place with His name, the unique name. The name in which we gather for the worship of God is a matter of great importance....Today Christians should be gathered together into only one name, the name of the Lord Jesus (Matt. 18:20). However, Christians are accustomed to being gathered into other names, such as Baptist, Presbyterian, Episcopalian, Lutheran, and Methodist. To be gathered into these different names is to be divided, because these names are the base of divisions....To have other names for our worship is an abomination; it is spiritual fornication. We are Christ's counterpart, His wife. Since we are His counterpart, we should not have a name other than His name.

Third, both Deuteronomy 12 and the New Testament reveal that the place chosen by God for our worship of Him is the place of His habitation....According to Ephesians 2:22, God's habitation, His dwelling place, is in our spirit. Yes, as a church we should be gathered into the name of Christ, but we also need to be exercised in our spirit. If we come together under the name of Christ but, instead of exercising our spirit, we remain in the natural mind or, even worse, in the flesh, we will not be in the habitation of God....We must be in the spirit. Otherwise, we will lose the proper ground of the church.

Fourth,...we must have the altar, which signifies the cross. Paul's word in 1 Corinthians 2:2 indicates the importance of this....The crucified Christ was the unique subject, the center, the content, and the substance of Paul's ministry....We should be on the cross...[and] not bring anything of the old man, anything of the flesh, the self, or the natural life, into the church. When we are on the cross, we are truly in the spirit.

If we have the name, the habitation, and the cross, there will be no divisions among us. No matter how many believers there may be in our locality and no matter how many meeting places, we all will be one. (*Life-study of Deuteronomy,* pp. 73-76)

Further Reading: Life-study of Deuteronomy, msg. 10; *CWWL, 1979,* vol. 2, "The Genuine Ground of Oneness," ch. 4

Enlightenment and inspiration:_____

_____

_____

_____

Morning Nourishment

Rev.   Saying, What you see write in a scroll and send *it*
1:11   to the seven churches: to Ephesus and to Smyrna
       and to Pergamos and to Thyatira and to Sardis
       and to Philadelphia and to Laodicea.
Matt. For where there are two or three gathered into
18:20 My name, there am I in their midst.   *Amen*

For convenience and practicality, we meet in the different cities where we live. Apparently we are divided by geography, for we meet in separate cities all over the world. Actually we remain in the oneness and are not divided, for wherever we may be, we meet in the Lord's name, in the spirit, and with the cross.

Recently, in the prayer meeting of the church in Anaheim, there were saints present from a number of different countries....Nobody gave a word about the subject of our prayer or about how we should pray. Nevertheless, we prayed in one accord. We could be one in such a way because, in spite of geographical separation, we all meet in the same place—in the Lord's name, in our spirit, and with the cross. (*Life-study of Deuteronomy*, p. 79)

Today's Reading

The situation with most Christians today is very different from this. They meet not in oneness but in many different denominations. Even if Christians from various denominations meet together, they may have difficulty praying together.... If the believers in Christ are to be one, they must give up all denominational things and simply come together in the name of the Lord Jesus, in the spirit, and with the cross. This is the oneness, and this is the proper ground for the worship of God.

Many Christians,...even though they may live in the same city,...will not meet together because they want to have their own preference. In the Lord's recovery, we care not for our preference but for the Lord's presence....Wherever we may be, in Anaheim or Taipei, in London or Tokyo, we should be gathered into the Lord's name [Matt. 18:20], and we should meet in our spirit and with the cross. If we all do this, we all will meet in the same place, although we meet in different localities. This one place is the ground of the unique oneness.

In the Lord's recovery, we have one name and one Spirit. We all meet in the name of Jesus Christ, and we all meet in the mingled spirit—in the regenerated human spirit indwelt by the Holy Spirit. We gather together in this spirit, not in our concept, desire, preference, or choice.... At the entrance of the church there is the cross, and in order to meet as the church we must experience the cross. The flesh, the self, and the natural man cannot be in the church; they must be crucified. Therefore, we meet in the name of the Lord Jesus, in the mingled spirit, and with the cross. This is the place where we meet, and here we have the oneness which we endeavor to keep in the unique name of the Lord. (*Life-study of Deuteronomy,* pp. 79-80)

One city may have many meeting halls or districts, but there is still only one church. In a large locality the church may meet in many different places, as did the church in Jerusalem (Acts 2:46-47). In the early days the saints met in their houses, but the meeting in each house was not a church. All the meetings in the different homes were the meetings of one church.... Although we may meet separately in several meeting halls on the Lord's Day morning, and although we have prayer meetings in several dozen homes, we are still one church with one administration and one testimony. Because there is only one church in the universe, there is only one expression of the church in any given place. This is the ground of the church. The church needs to keep the principle of having one church for one place, one city with only one church; otherwise, the church will be divided. (*CWWL, 1966,* vol. 3, "The Revelation of Christ and the Reality of the Church," p. 215)

Further Reading: Life-study of Deuteronomy, msg. 11; *CWWL, 1966,* vol. 3, pp. 213-226

*Enlightenment and inspiration:*_____
_____
_____
_____

Morning Nourishment

1 Cor.   To the church of God which is in Corinth, to
1:2   those who have been sanctified in Christ Jesus,
         ...with all those who call upon the name of our
         Lord Jesus Christ in every place...
2 Chron.   ...I have not chosen a city out of all the tribes
6:5-6   of Israel to build a house for My name that it
           might be there;...but I have chosen Jerusalem
           that My name might be there...

The church is constituted of the universal God, but it exists on earth in many localities, one of which was Corinth. In nature the church is universal in God, but in practice the church is local in a definite place. Hence, the church has two aspects: the universal and the local. Without the universal aspect, the church is void of content; without the local aspect, it is impossible for the church to have any expression and practice. Hence, the New Testament stresses the local aspect of the church also (Acts 8:1; 13:1; Rev. 1:11; etc.). (1 Cor. 1:2, footnote 2)

Our enjoyment of Christ has two aspects. One aspect is individual, which can be enjoyed in any place. The other aspect is corporate. If we desire to worship God with all the saints,... we cannot do it according to our desire, but according to God's ordination. The place appointed by God was eventually Jerusalem (2 Chron. 6:5-6; John 4:20). Jerusalem became the unique worship center chosen by God, which helped to maintain and preserve the oneness among the children of Israel for generations. (*CWWL, 1966,* vol. 3, "The Revelation of Christ and the Reality of the Church," pp. 219-220)

Today's Reading

The church of God [in 1 Corinthians 1:2a]...indicates that the church is not only being possessed by God, but it has God as its nature and essence, which are divine, general, universal, and eternal....God is the nature and essence of the church. Therefore, the church is divine.

"The church...in Corinth" (v. 2b) was a church in a city, remaining in a definite locality and taking it as its standing, ground, and jurisdiction for its administration in business affairs. As such, it was physical, particular, local, and temporal in time. The church of God to whom Paul wrote was not in the heavens but in Corinth....The church remained in that locality for a local testimony of Christ. A local testimony of Christ is a part of the universal testimony of Christ. The universal testimony is composed of and constituted with the local testimonies.

The standing, ground, and jurisdiction of the church is physical rather than divine, particular rather than general, local rather than universal, and temporal in time rather than eternal. These are the local aspects of the church.

The church is "sanctified in Christ" (v. 2c), having been sanctified, made holy, in Christ, who is the embodiment of the processed Triune God in His fullness, as its element and sphere.

The church is composed of the "called saints" (v. 2d)—the assembly of the saints, the sanctified ones, who have been called out of the satanic world. We have been called by God to be sanctified in Christ. We are no longer in the world; we are in the church, which is called by God and sanctified in a wonderful person, Christ, who is our element within and our sphere without.

Verse 2 contains five qualifications for a genuine church. ...The church which is genuine is the church of God, it is the church in a locality, it is sanctified in Christ, and it is composed of the called saints. Verse 2e continues with the fifth qualification: "With all those who call upon the name of our Lord Jesus Christ in every place." This...indicates that the church which is genuine is related with all the saints who call upon the name of the Lord Jesus Christ in every place around the globe...including the believers today, those who came before us, and those who will come after us—who call upon the name of our Lord Jesus Christ in every place. (*A Genuine Church* (booklet), pp. 7-11)

Further Reading: CWWL, 1990, vol. 2, "A Genuine Church," pp. 373-382; *The Ground of the Church* (booklet)

Enlightenment and inspiration:_____

_____

_____

_____

Morning Nourishment

Psa. Beautiful in elevation, the joy of the whole earth,
48:2 is Mount Zion, the sides of the north, the city of
the great King.

11-12 Let Mount Zion rejoice; let the daughters of
Judah exult because of Your judgments. Walk
about Zion, and go around her; count her towers.

Zion was the city of King David (2 Sam. 5:7), the center
of the city of Jerusalem, where the temple as God's dwelling
place on earth was built (Psa. 9:11; 74:2; 76:2b; 135:21; Isa.
8:18). Zion within Jerusalem typifies the body of overcomers,
the perfected and matured God-men, within the church as the
heavenly Jerusalem (Heb. 12:22; Rev. 14:1-5). As the highlight and beauty of the holy city Jerusalem (Psa. 48:2; 50:2),
Zion typifies the overcomers as the high peak, the center, the
uplifting, the strengthening, the enriching, the beauty, and
the reality of the church (48:2, 11-12; 20:2; 53:6a; 87:2). The
overcomers as Zion are the reality of the Body of Christ and
consummate the building up of the Body in the local churches
to bring in the consummated holy city, New Jerusalem, the
Holy of Holies as God's dwelling place, in eternity (Rev. 21:1-3,
16, 22). In the new heaven and new earth the entire New
Jerusalem will become Zion, with all the believers as overcomers (Rev. 21:7 and footnote 1). (Psa. 48:2, footnote 1)

Today's Reading

The church life is the right place for you to be an overcomer.
But this does not mean that as long as you are in the church
life, you are an overcomer. It is one thing to be in the church life.
It is another thing to be an overcomer in the church life.

In the Old Testament there was the city of Jerusalem
with Zion as the center....The church life is today's Jerusalem; within the church life there must be a group of overcomers, and these overcomers are today's Zion. According to
Revelation 14, the overcomers are standing on Mount Zion
with the Lord (vv. 1-5). Actually, in typology the overcomers
are today's Zion....Without Zion (the overcomers), Jerusalem

(the church life) cannot be kept and maintained.

Zion is the high peak, the center, the uplifting, the strengthening, the enriching, and the reality of the church, the holy city. If there are no overcomers in a local church, that church is like Jerusalem without Zion.... A local church must have some overcomers, and these overcomers are the peak and the center of that local church. They are the uplifting, the strengthening, the enriching, and the reality of that local church....Once a church has some full-time workers as overcomers, that church is like Jerusalem with the peak of Zion. The overcomers as Zion are the highlight, the center, and the reality of the church.

The overcomers as today's Zion are for the consummation of the holy city (the church). They are to consummate, to finish, the building up of the local church and to bring in the consummated New Jerusalem in eternity (21:1-2). In order to complete the building up of the Body, the Lord needs the overcomers, and the building up of the Body consummates in the New Jerusalem. This is why at the end of the Bible, in the last book, there is the calling for the overcomers. Today the way to become vitalized is to answer the Lord's call to be an overcomer.

There are two ways before us today. We can either choose to be vitalized or choose not to be vitalized. I am presenting these two ways before us. Which way will we take? Are we going to be vitalized or not? We have to make a resolution. In Judges 5:15 Deborah said, "Among the divisions of Reuben / There were great resolutions in heart." We have to make a resolution to be the overcomers, the vitalized ones. An overcomer overcomes anything that replaces Christ or that is against Christ. In the Bible there is the age of the overcomers, and there is the calling for the overcomers. Furthermore, there is a way for us to be vitalized so that we can be the overcomers. (*CWWL, 1993,* vol. 2, "The Training and the Practice of the Vital Groups," pp. 274-275)

Further Reading: CWWL, 1993, vol. 2, "The Training and the Practice of the Vital Groups," ch. 1

Enlightenment and inspiration:_____

_____

_____

_____

Morning Nourishment

Deut. **Yet you may slaughter and eat meat within all**
12:15 **your gates...according to the blessing of Jeho-**
vah your God which He has given you...

16:16 **Three times a year all your males shall appear**
before Jehovah your God in the place which He
will choose....And they shall not appear before
Jehovah empty-handed.

The children of Israel could enjoy the rich produce of the good land in two ways. The common way was to enjoy the common portion of the rich produce of the good land at any time, in any place, and with anybody. The special way was to enjoy the top portion, the firstfruit and the firstborn, in the unique place chosen by God.

If we consider our experience, we shall see that we have two kinds of enjoyment of Christ's riches....We may say that we have the common enjoyment of Christ and the special enjoyment of Christ. We have experienced the special enjoyment of Christ in the proper church life. Whenever we come to a meeting of the church, the enjoyment of Christ is high and rich. We all need to enjoy Christ both in our private life and in the church life. Although the enjoyment of Christ in the church life is wonderful, it cannot replace our enjoyment of Him in our private life. Likewise, the enjoyment in our private life cannot replace the enjoyment in our public life, in our church life. Many Christians today do not see these two aspects of the enjoyment of Christ. (*CWWL, 1975-1976,* vol. 3, "Young People's Training," pp. 454-455)

Today's Reading

The life we need to enjoy the good land...is a life first of all of laboring on Christ,...seeking to enjoy Him and experience Him in every situation.

The people of Israel after they occupied the good land and all their enemies were subdued...simply labored on the land. They tilled the ground, sowed the seed, watered the plants, nurtured the vines, and pruned the trees....It is a picture of how we must work diligently on Christ that we may enjoy His all-inclusive riches.

Christ is rich beyond measure, but the church today is groveling in poverty. Why? It is because the Lord's children today are indolent. They will not exert themselves to labor on Christ.

The Lord told His people that they must come together to worship Him at least three times a year....And He told them that whenever they come together...they must bring something in their hands to Him...of the produce of the good land. If they were lazy and did not work on the land, not only would they be unable to bring anything to the Lord, but they would have nothing to satisfy themselves; they would be hungry.

We have to labor on Christ day by day so that we produce Him in mass production. We need more than just a little of Christ to satisfy our own needs. We must produce enough of Him so that there will be a surplus remaining for others.

We are meeting together to have an exhibition of Christ, not just the Christ whom God gave us but the Christ we have produced, the Christ upon whom we have labored and whom we have experienced....Brothers and sisters, this is what all our meetings should be—an exhibition, a fair, in which all sorts of the produce of Christ are displayed.

The life in the land is a life full of the enjoyment of Christ, both personally and collectively with the Lord's people. May we be diligent to labor on Him, to have our hands filled with Him, and then come to the place that He has appointed, to the very ground of unity, to enjoy this rich and glorious Christ with God's children and with God Himself. (*CWWL, 1961-1962,* vol. 4, "The All-inclusive Christ," pp. 342-344, 347, 352)

Further Reading: CWWL, 1963, vol. 4, "The Life and Way for the Practice of the Church Life," chs. 14-15; *CWWL, 1961-1962,* vol. 4, "The All-inclusive Christ," chs. 15-16; *CWWL, 1975-1976,* vol. 3, "Young People's Training," chs. 12-13

*Enlightenment and inspiration:*_____

_____

_____

_____

Morning Nourishment

Col. And He is the Head of the Body, the church; He is
1:18 the beginning, the Firstborn from the dead, that
He Himself might have the first place in all things.

3:11 Where there cannot be Greek and Jew, circumcision and uncircumcision, barbarian, Scythian,
slave, free man, but Christ is all and in all.

Often the pagan centers of worship were located on
mountains or hills or under flourishing trees (Deut. 12:2).
The mountains and hills signify the exaltation of something
other than Christ, and the flourishing trees signify things
that are beautiful and attractive. The various worship centers
in today's Christianity lift up something other than Christ. In
principle, these centers of worship are on a mountain or hill,
the high places. However, God's people were to come to Mount
Zion, the unique place chosen by God for corporate worship.
The worship at the high places was a factor in the dispersion
of the children of Israel.

In principle, we must destroy all the places, idols, and
names. To do this is to do what is right in the eyes of the Lord.
But if we insist on our own choice, we are doing what is right
in our own eyes. We must fear the Lord and go to the place He
has chosen. (*CWWL, 1979*, vol. 2, "The Genuine Ground of
Oneness," p. 273)

Today's Reading

The ground of oneness is not simply a matter of one city,
one church. The ground of oneness is deeper, richer, higher,
and fuller than this. We all must learn that in this universe
God has chosen only one place, and that place is the church.

The church with Christ is the unique place of God's choice.
In order to fulfill the word of Colossians 3:11, every other
place must be utterly destroyed. We must destroy everything
that is not the church with Christ. Then we will simply be in
the church life enjoying Christ as the riches of the good land.
As we enjoy Him with God, we will be planted in the house
of the Lord, we will grow, and we will flourish. This is the

proper way to have the Christian life and the church life. This is the ground of oneness.

On this ground it is not possible to have division, for the basis of division has been destroyed. Our temperament, disposition, natural characteristics, and preferences have all been eliminated. Our religion, culture, and particular ways have also been destroyed.

In the church there cannot be anything other than Christ. Christ must be all and in all.... As we enjoy Him before God, this enjoyment will become our worship, our church life, and even our Christian daily living. Then we will grow and mature on the ground of oneness.

From my experience in the Lord's recovery...I can testify that the unique place of God's choice leaves no opportunity for the indulgence of lust or for the exercise of our ambition. During all the years in China, I was under the direction of Brother Nee's ministry. In all my preaching I was the same as he. All the "high places" were torn down, and therefore there was no room for the indulgence of lust or the carrying out of selfish ambition. The same is true among us today. We care only to exalt Christ. If we maintain the ground of oneness, God's unique choice, without elevating anything other than Christ, it will not be possible to have division. In the Lord's recovery we elevate Christ and Christ alone. We may talk a great deal about life, but we do not even elevate life to the point of making it a high place. Certain brothers among us are very keen and have a good deal of natural ability. But their keenness and ability must be restricted by the ground of God's choice. This restriction will keep them from elevating something in place of Christ. We in the Lord's recovery can testify that, in contrast to today's Christianity, we have no high places. (*CWWL, 1979,* vol. 2, "The Genuine Ground of Oneness," pp. 288-289, 320-321)

Further Reading: CWWL, 1979, vol. 2, "The Genuine Ground of Oneness," chs. 5, 8, 10; *CWWL, 1968,* vol. 1, "The Practical Expression of the Church," ch. 9

*Enlightenment and inspiration:*_____

_____
_____
_____

Hymns, #1265

1 The churches are the Body
   Of Christ on earth today.
   They are His testimony,
   That He may have a way.
   They are the golden lampstands
   In cities far and wide.
   They are His fighting army,
   And His beloved bride.

   The churches, the churches,
   Upon the earth today;
   Lord, stir our hearts for Thy desire,
   And build us, oh, build us, Lord,
       we pray.

2 Oh, how we need the churches,
   All of them, great or small!
   We need their many portions
   To profit us withal.
   Yes, Lord, enlarge the churches;
   We love their needs to bear.
   Enlarge our hearts, Lord Jesus,
   In fellowship and prayer.

3 The Lord's eyes o'er the whole earth
   Are running to and fro;
   Those seven, burning, searching,
   Our heart's desire to know.
   His purpose—many churches,
   Built up in one accord;
   This golden testimony
   Will thus express the Lord.

4 And soon will be the coming
   Of our triumphant King!
   He's coming for the churches
   Where His sweet praises ring.
   Come, Lord, come reap the firstfruits,
   As draws the harvest nigh,
   And to Thy throne do take us,
   To reign with Thee on high.

*Composition for prophecy with main point and sub-points:*_____

_____
_____
_____
_____
_____
_____
_____
_____
_____
_____
_____
_____
_____
_____
_____
_____
_____
_____
_____
_____
_____
_____
_____
_____
_____
_____
_____
_____
_____
_____
_____
_____
_____
_____
_____
_____

Avoiding Division,
Which Is versus the Oneness That We Keep,
and Rejecting Apostasy,
Which Is versus the Faith That We Contend For

Scripture Reading: Deut. 12—13; Psa. 133; John 17:21-23; Eph.
4:3-6; Jude 1-3, 19-21

Day 1

I. **According to Moses' word in Deuteronomy 12
and 13, we must avoid division and reject apostasy:**
   A. We must keep the unique oneness of God's people
   and the unique faith in the person and redemptive
   work of Christ.
   B. Apostasy in the Old Testament denotes giving up
   God and turning away from God to idols; in the New
   Testament apostasy is heresy, denoting the denial
   of Christ's deity and not believing that Jesus Christ
   is God incarnated to be a man—John 1:1, 14; 1 John
   2:18, 22; 4:2-3.
   C. Apostasy, or heresy, insults and damages the person
   of Christ, and division destroys the Body of Christ
   as Christ's corporate expression; thus, apostasy and
   division damage the entire economy of God.
   D. Because of this, the apostle Paul charges us to turn
   away from the divisive ones (Rom. 16:17), and the
   apostle John enjoins us to reject the heretical ones
   (2 John 9-11).
   E. Like Moses in Deuteronomy and the apostles in the
   New Testament, we must be very strict concerning
   division and apostasy; we must keep the unique oneness of God's people and the unique faith in the person and redemptive work of Christ—Eph. 4:3, 13.

Day 2

II. **Division is all-inclusive; it includes all negative
things, such as Satan, sin, worldliness, the flesh,**

the self, the old man, and evil temper—Rom.
16:17-18; Titus 3:10:

A. We should not think that division stands by itself
and is not related to the flesh, the self, and worldliness—Gal. 5:19-21; Matt. 16:23-24; 1 John 2:15-16.

B. If we are enlightened concerning the nature of division, we will see that it is not only related to all negative things but includes all negative things.

C. To be in division is to be in death; Christianity is
filled with death and darkness because the genuine oneness in life is lacking.

D. Divisions come out of different teachings, teachings other than God's economy—1 Tim. 1:3-4:

1. Whatever we teach should not be measured by
whether it is wrong or right; it must be measured
by whether it is divisive or not; only one kind of
ministry builds up and never divides—this is
the unique ministry of God's economy.

2. It kills people to teach differently; to teach differently tears down God's building and annuls
God's entire economy; we all must realize that
even a small amount of teaching in a different
way destroys the recovery.

3. The only way that can preserve us in the recovery is the unique ministry; if we say that we are
in the recovery, yet we teach something so lightly,
even in a concealed way, that is different from
God's economy, we sow the seed that will grow
up in division; therefore, the only way that we
can be preserved in the eternal oneness is to
teach the same thing in God's economy.

4. The different teachings of the dissenting ones
are winds used by God's enemy to distract His
people and carry them away from His economy—
Eph. 4:14.

5. The dividing teachings are organized and systematized by Satan to cause serious error and
thus damage the practical oneness of the Body
life—v. 14.

6. The different teachings are the major source of the church's decline, degradation, and deterioration—1 Tim. 1:3-4, 6-7; 6:3-5, 20-21.

E. The apostles taught the same thing to all the saints in all the places and in all the churches—1 Cor. 4:17; 7:17; 11:16; 14:33b-34:
 1. We also must teach the same thing in all the churches in every country throughout the earth—Matt. 28:19-20.
 2. There is no thought in the New Testament that a teaching is good for one church but not for the other churches; rather, the New Testament reveals that all the churches were the same in receiving the teachings—Titus 1:9.

III. **The genuine oneness is an all-inclusive, comprehensive oneness that includes all positive things—Psa. 23:6; 36:8-9; 43:3-4; 84:1-8, 10-12; 92:10; 133:1, 3b:**
 A. The Lord has given us the glory that the Father has given Him so that we may be one in the Father and in the Son; this points to a oneness in the divine nature and the Divine Being; oneness is actually the mingling of the processed and consummated Triune God with the believers—John 17:21-23; Eph. 4:3-6.
 B. When the oneness is recovered, all the spiritual riches and all the positive things are recovered with it, because they all exist in the oneness—v. 3; 3:8:
 1. All the godly things and all the spiritual riches are ours on the genuine ground of oneness—Deut. 8:7-9; 12:12, 26-28.
 2. The genuine oneness is not a partial oneness; it is a great, complete, comprehensive oneness, a oneness in entirety.
 C. Psalm 133 is a psalm on the oneness that includes all positive attributes and virtues; if we see the vision of the oneness of entirety, all the germs of division will be killed, and we will be delivered from every kind of division.

Day 4

D. For the recovery and preservation of the genuine, all-inclusive oneness, we must destroy the high places—1 Kings 11:7-8; 12:26-33; 13:33-34; 14:22-23; 15:14; 22:43; 2 Kings 12:2-3; 14:3-4; 15:3-4, 34-35:

1. In His wisdom God required His people to destroy all the places in which the nations served their gods; to set up a high place is to have a division; hence, the significance of high places is division—Deut. 12:1-3.

2. To preserve the oneness of His people, God required that they come to the unique place of His choice; the high places were a substitute and an alternative for this unique place—vv. 8, 11, 13-14, 18.

3. A high place is an elevation, something lifted above the common level; in principle, every high place, every division, involves the uplifting, the exaltation, of something other than Christ—cf. Col. 1:18.

4. The record of the building of the high places under Solomon and Jeroboam has a spiritual significance; it was written for our spiritual instruction—Rom. 15:4-6:

    a. According to this record, division is caused by lust and ambition; Solomon is an example of the former, and Jeroboam is an example of the latter.

    b. The high places built by Solomon and Jeroboam seriously damaged the ground of oneness—1 Kings 11:7-8; 12:26-33.

    c. In the church life we should not have any high places; instead, we should all be on one level to exalt Christ—Col. 1:18; 3:10-11.

    d. The divisions in Christianity are caused by selfishness and ambition—Phil. 2:21; 3 John 9-10; Rom. 16:17-18; 1 Kings 12:26-33.

5. Spiritually speaking, we must destroy every place other than the church and every name other than the name of Christ; this means that we must destroy our culture, disposition, temperament, habits, natural characteristics, preferences, and religious background with its influence—everything that damages the genuine oneness—Gal. 2:20; 5:24; 6:14.

Day 5

E. In the Lord's recovery we elevate Christ and Christ alone—Col. 1:18:
   1. We can testify that, in contrast to today's Christianity, we have no high places.
   2. Having come to the church, we should have no "high places," elevations where something other than Christ is uplifted; we should have nothing other than the person of Christ and the unique way of the cross—1 Cor. 1:30; 2:4; Col. 1:20; 2:11; 3:11.
   3. In the church we enjoy Christ as the rich produce of the land; our enjoyment of Christ in the presence of God becomes our worship, our church life, and even our Christian living, and we grow and mature on the ground of oneness—Eph. 3:8; 4:3, 14-16.

IV. **We must be fully exercised to separate ourselves from any heresy (apostasy) and heretics (apostates):**
   A. Heretics do not confess that Jesus is God incarnate (not confessing that He has come in the flesh through the divine conception of the Holy Spirit); thus, they deny the deity of Christ—1 John 4:3; 2 John 7; cf. Luke 1:31-35; John 20:28-29; Rom. 9:5.
   B. The Spirit works in the believers to confess to them that Christ came in the flesh—1 John 4:1-2:
      1. Anyone who rejects Christ's incarnation and thereby rejects His redemption also denies Christ's resurrection.

  2. If anyone denies Christ's incarnation, that one denies Christ's holy birth, humanity, human living, redemption through crucifixion, and resurrection; this utterly annuls the enjoyment of the life-giving Spirit as the reality of the processed Triune God—2:23.

 C. A heretic is one who denies the divine conception and deity of Christ, as today's modernists do; such a one we must reject, not receiving him into our house nor greeting him; thus, we will not have any contact with him or any share in his heresy, heresy that is blasphemous to God and contagious like leprosy—2 Pet. 2:1-3; 2 John 10.

 D. Just as bringing to others the divine truth of the wonderful Christ is an excellent deed (Rom. 10:15), so spreading the satanic heresy, which defiles the glorious deity of Christ, is an evil work; it is a blasphemy and abomination to God; it is also a damage and curse to men.

 E. No one who is a believer in Christ and a child of God should have any share in this evil! Even to greet such an evil one is prohibited! A severe and clear separation from this evil should be maintained!— 2 John 8-11.

Day 6

V. **Jude exhorts us to earnestly contend for the faith—Jude 1-3:**

 A. "The faith" in Jude is not subjective faith as our believing but objective faith as our belief, referring to the things we believe in, the contents of the New Testament as our faith, in which we believe for our common salvation—Acts 6:7; 1 Tim. 1:19; 3:9; 4:1; 5:8; 6:10, 21; 2 Tim. 3:8; 4:7; Titus 1:13.

 B. Our Christian faith is composed of our belief concerning six basic items: the Bible, God, Christ, the work of Christ, salvation, and the church—Eph. 4:13:

1. The Bible, word by word, is divinely inspired by God, as the breath of God—2 Pet. 1:21; 2 Tim. 3:16.
2. God is uniquely one but triune—the Father, the Son, and the Spirit—Matt. 3:16-17; 28:19; 2 Cor. 13:14; Eph. 2:18; 3:14-17; Rev. 1:4-5.
3. Christ was the very God in eternity (John 1:1) and became a man in time (v. 14); His deity is complete, and His humanity is perfect; hence, He is both God and man (20:28; Rom. 9:5; John 19:5; 1 Tim. 2:5), possessing both divinity and humanity.
4. Christ first became a man in incarnation (John 1:14) and died on the cross for our redemption (1 Pet. 2:24; Rev. 5:9); then He rose from the dead for our regeneration (1 Pet. 1:3), ascended to the heavens to be the Lord of all (Acts 2:33, 36; 10:36), and will come back as the Bridegroom to the church (John 3:29; Rev. 19:7) and the King of kings to all the nations (v. 16); these are the main aspects of the work of Christ.
5. A sinner must repent to God (Acts 2:38; 26:20) and believe into Christ (John 3:16; Acts 16:31) for forgiveness of sins (10:43), for redemption (Rom. 3:24), for justification (Acts 13:39), and for regeneration (John 3:6) in order that he may have eternal life (v. 36) to become a child of God (1:12) and a member of Christ (1 Cor. 12:27); this is our salvation through faith (Eph. 2:4-9).
6. The church, composed of all the genuine believers in Christ, as the Body of Christ (1:22-23; Col. 1:24), is universally one (Eph. 4:4), and a local church as the expression of the Body of Christ is locally one—one city, one church (Rev. 1:11):
   a. This does not mean, however, that a real believer in Christ who does not agree with one city, one church is not saved; he or she is saved, but there is something lacking, not for salvation but for the proper church life.

b. By standing on the proper ground of the church, we are choosing to love all the brothers, not only those who are meeting with us.

C. This faith, not any doctrine, has been delivered once for all to the saints; for this faith we should earnestly contend—1 Tim. 6:12.

D. We build up ourselves upon the foundation of this most holy faith by enjoying the entire Blessed Trinity so that we may become the New Jerusalem as the totality of the eternal life—Jude 19-21; cf. John 4:14b.

E. The entire Blessed Trinity is employed and enjoyed by us as we exercise our spirit by "praying in the Holy Spirit" to keep ourselves "in the love of God, awaiting the mercy of our Lord Jesus Christ unto eternal life"—Jude 20-21:

1. *Unto eternal life* (v. 21), or *into eternal life* (John 4:14b), is a particular expression; *unto,* or *into,* speaks of destination and also means "to become."

2. By exercising our spirit to enjoy the Blessed Trinity and contend for the faith, we become the New Jerusalem as the totality of the eternal life—Rev. 22:1-2a; 21:10-11.

Morning Nourishment

Deut.   You shall not listen to the words of that prophet
13:3-4   or to that dreamer of dreams; for Jehovah your
         God is testing you in order to know whether you
         love Jehovah your God with all your heart and
         with all your soul. You shall follow Jehovah your
         God; and you shall fear Him, keep His command-
         ments, listen to His voice, serve Him, and hold
         fast to Him.

In Deuteronomy 12 Moses was strict in the matter of division, and in Deuteronomy 13 he was strict in the matter of
apostasy.

In the Old Testament, apostasy denotes the giving up of
God and the turning away from God to idols. In the New Testament, apostasy denotes the denial of Christ's deity; it refers
to not believing that Christ is God incarnated to be a man.
(*Life-study of Deuteronomy,* pp. 86, 81)

Today's Reading

We need to be clear regarding the difference between teaching apostasy and being wrong in doctrine. Someone may not be
correct in his teaching about a certain doctrine, but this does
not mean that he is apostate. For example, suppose a brother
in the Lord, a genuine believer in Christ, is somewhat mis-
taken in his teaching regarding the rapture.... According to
the New Testament, someone becomes apostate not by teaching incorrectly about the rapture but by giving up the faith
that Jesus Christ is God and that He came in the flesh to be
a man.

In Romans 14 and 15 Paul is generous, broad-minded, and
all-embracing, but in Romans 16:17 he is very narrow and
strict. "I exhort you, brothers, to mark those who make divisions and causes of stumbling contrary to the teaching which
you have learned, and turn away from them." On the one
hand, we need to receive all kinds of genuine believers; on the
other hand, we need to be narrow and strict in dealing with
divisive ones. In 16:17 Paul does not say, "These divisive ones

are brothers. We need to receive them and love them." No, he tells us to mark them and to turn away from them. To turn away from those who make divisions and causes of falling is to quarantine them.

Like the apostles in the New Testament,...we also must be very strict concerning division and apostasy. This means that we must keep the unique oneness of God's people and the unique faith in the person and redemptive work of Christ.

The New Testament term for apostasy is *heresy*. Apostasy and heresy are an insult to the person of God. In the Old Testament the apostates turned away from God and followed idols....In the New Testament the heretics denied that Jesus Christ is God incarnated to become a man. Such a denial is heresy, New Testament apostasy. This heresy damages the person of Christ. In both the Old Testament and the New Testament, God does not tolerate apostasy or heresy.

The Lord hates division because it destroys His people as His expression. In the Old Testament the children of Israel were God's people for His corporate expression. In the New Testament the corporate expression of the Lord is the Body of Christ. Whereas heresy insults and damages the person of Christ, division damages the Body of Christ. Division kills the Body of Christ and cuts it into pieces. Because heresy damages the Head and because division kills the Body, the Lord, in both the New Testament and the Old Testament, will never tolerate heresy and division.

Instead of sympathizing with those who make divisions and causes of falling, we are charged by Paul to turn away from them. The reason we must turn away from those who cause divisions is that division is extremely serious—it destroys the Body of Christ....Apostasy and division damage the entire economy of God. (*Life-study of Deuteronomy,* pp. 82-84, 86-89)

Further Reading: Life-study of Deuteronomy, msgs. 12-13; *CWWL, 1979,* vol. 2, "The Genuine Ground of Oneness," chs. 1, 4

Enlightenment and inspiration:_____

_____

_____

_____

Morning Nourishment

Eph. That we may be no longer little children tossed
4:14 by waves and carried about by every wind of
teaching in the sleight of men, in craftiness with
a view to a system of error.

1 Tim. Even as I exhorted you...to remain in Ephesus in
1:3-4 order that you might charge certain ones not to
teach different things...which produce questionings rather than God's economy, which is in faith.

The dividing teachings are organized and systematized by
Satan to cause serious error and thus damage the practical
oneness of the Body life. The sleight is of men, but the system
of error is of Satan and is related to the deceitful teachings
that are designed by the evil one to distract the saints from
Christ and the church life. (Eph. 4:14, footnote 5)

Never regard division as an insignificant matter....To be
in oneness is to be in life, but to be in division is to be in death.

Division is all-inclusive. It comprises such negative things
as Satan, sin, worldliness, the flesh, the self, the old man, and
evil temper. If we are enlightened concerning the nature of
division, we will see that it includes every negative thing.
Do not think that division stands by itself and that it is not
related to such things as the flesh, the self, and worldliness.
Division is not only related to all negative things; it includes
all negative things. (*CWWL, 1979*, vol. 2, "The Genuine Ground
of Oneness," pp. 253-254)

Today's Reading

Throughout the twenty centuries of church history, the
divisions, confusions, and problems that have taken place
among all the Christians were all due to a ministry....All the
different kinds of Christian groups come out of different min-
istries. A ministry is mainly a teaching. We must realize that
the teaching that a Christian teaches ministers something....
A teaching always issues in something. Based upon the issue
of your teaching, your teaching may be considered as a ministry....To serve others with something is to minister.

Poison after poison was injected into the Christian church while the church was going on. At the conclusion of his writing ministry, Paul wrote 1 Timothy to inoculate the church against all these poisons....This phrase *not to teach different things* [1:3] seems so simple....We may not think that this is serious, but actually it is more than serious. It kills people to teach differently. To teach differently tears down God's building and annuls God's entire economy. We all must realize that even a small amount of teaching in a different way destroys the recovery. There is a proverb that says, "One sentence can build up the nation, and one sentence can destroy the entire nation."...Just speaking one sentence that conveys your kind of concept tears down everything.

The only way that can preserve us in the recovery is the unique ministry. If we say that we are in the recovery, yet we teach something so lightly, even in a concealed way, that is different from God's economy, we sow the seed that will grow up in division. Therefore, the only way that we can be preserved in the eternal oneness is to teach the same thing, God's economy. This kind of teaching is called the New Testament ministry, the ministry of the new covenant. The ministry of the new covenant is to minister only the processed Triune God to be dispensed into His chosen people as life and life supply to produce members of Christ to form the Body to express the Triune God. This is the New Testament economy. To teach anything, even good things and scriptural things, that is even a little apart from God's New Testament economy will still issue in division, and that will be very much used by the subtle one, the evil one. We must, therefore, be on the alert. (*CWWL, 1984,* vol. 2, "Elders' Training, Book 3: The Way to Carry Out the Vision," pp. 267-268, 273)

Further Reading: CWWL, 1979, vol. 2, "The Genuine Ground of Oneness," chs. 3, 9; *CWWL, 1984,* vol. 2, "Elders' Training, Book 3: The Way to Carry Out the Vision," ch. 4

Enlightenment and inspiration:_____

_____

_____

_____

Morning Nourishment

1 Cor.   Because of this I have sent Timothy to you, who
  4:17   is my beloved and faithful child in the Lord, who
        will remind you of my ways which are in Christ,
        even as I teach everywhere in every church.
11:16   But if anyone seems to be contentious, we do
        not have such a custom *of being so,* neither the
        churches of God.

Oneness is all-inclusive. It includes God, Christ, and the Spirit....In the oneness revealed in [Ephesians 4:3-6], we have God the Father, Christ the Lord, and the Spirit as the Giver of life. This oneness includes such positive things as our regenerated spirit and our transformed and renewed mind. Everything positive is included in the proper oneness. (*CWWL, 1979,* vol. 2, "The Genuine Ground of Oneness," p. 254)

Today's Reading

Our practice of oneness is based upon the attribute of the oneness of the church: one Spirit, one Lord, one God, one Body, one faith, one baptism, and one hope [Eph. 4:4-6]....Moreover, the practice of this oneness is according to the apostles' teaching (1 Cor. 4:17b; 7:17b; 11:16; 14:34a). The apostles taught the same thing to all the saints in all the places and in all the churches. At the same time, the practice of this oneness is also according to the same speaking of the Spirit to the churches (Rev. 2:7, 11a, 17a, 29; 3:6, 13, 22). The seven epistles to the seven churches in Revelation 2 and 3 are words spoken to all the churches....All the churches have the same Bible, and everyone is practicing oneness according to the same speaking. Finally, the practice of oneness indicates that the seven churches as the seven lampstands are completely identical (1:20)....Although they are distinct and self-contained, they are completely identical in nature, shape, function, and expression. (*CWWL, 1990,* vol. 2, "The Oneness and the One Accord according to the Lord's Aspiration and the Body Life and Service according to His Pleasure," pp. 74-75)

The reason for this oneness is that God Himself is one. Oneness is His nature. In all God's acts we see one origin, one element, and one essence. In God's creation we see one God and one corporate man. In His selection we also have the one God and one man. Moreover, in the church we have the one Spirit and one new man. Eventually, in the New Jerusalem we have the unique Triune God in the one city characterized by the one throne, the one street, the one river, and the one tree. Therefore, the oneness about which we are speaking is not a partial oneness; it is a great, complete, comprehensive oneness, a oneness in entirety....If we see the vision of the oneness of entirety, all the germs of division will be killed, and we will be delivered from every kind of division.

The oneness [in John 17:21-23] is not merely that of individual units coming together in harmony and agreement. Here the Lord said that He has given us the very glory the Father has given Him in order that we may be one in the Father and the Son. This points to a oneness that exists in the divine nature and the Divine Being. The three of the Triune God are one in Their nature and being. The oneness of the believers in Christ should be essentially the same.

[In Ephesians 4:4-6] Paul speaks of the Body and of the one Spirit, the one Lord, and the one God and Father. The fact that the Body and the Triune God are mentioned together indicates that oneness is actually the mingling of the Triune God with the believers.

When we come back to the oneness, all the godly, heavenly, spiritual things return...[and] are ours on the ground of oneness. (*CWWL, 1979,* vol. 2, "The Genuine Ground of Oneness," pp. 243, 292-293, 330)

Further Reading: CWWL, 1978, vol. 3, "Truth Messages," ch. 7; *CWWL, 1990,* vol. 2, "The Intrinsic Problem in the Lord's Recovery Today and Its Scriptural Remedy," chs. 1-2

Enlightenment and inspiration:_____

_____
_____
_____

Morning Nourishment

Col. And He is the Head of the Body, the church; He is
1:18 the beginning, the Firstborn from the dead, that
He Himself might have the first place in all things.
3:10-11 And have put on the new man...where there cannot be Greek and Jew, circumcision and uncircumcision, barbarian, Scythian, slave, free man, but Christ is all and in all.

In Deuteronomy 12 Moses charged the children of Israel to "completely destroy all the places where the nations...have served their gods, on the high mountains and on the hills and under every flourishing tree" (v. 2). He also charged them to tear down their altars...(v. 3). Having destroyed all these things, they were to come to the unique place of God's choice. According to 1 Kings, the temple was built in Jerusalem, the place God had chosen,...a unique place for His presence. This one place protected God's people from division.

Although the children of Israel destroyed the places wherein the nations served their gods,...eventually the very things that had been destroyed came back....In fact, Solomon, the very one who built the temple according to God's desire on the ground of oneness, took the lead to build up the high places once again (1 Kings 11:6-8). (*CWWL, 1979,* vol. 2, "The Genuine Ground of Oneness," p. 313)

Today's Reading

To set up a high place is to have a division. Hence, the significance of high places is division....To preserve the oneness of His people, God required that they come to the unique place of His choice. The high places, however, were a substitute and an alternative for this unique place....The unique place, Jerusalem, signifies oneness, whereas the high places signify division. Just as all manner of evil and abominable things were related to the setting up of the high places, so, in New Testament terms, all manner of evil is related to division.

According to the record in 1 Kings, two kings...took the

lead to set up the high places. In the case of Solomon, the building of the high places was related to the indulgence of lust. Solomon had hundreds of wives and concubines....His wives had "turned his heart after other gods" (11:4). In the case of Jeroboam, the building of the high places was related to ambition (12:26-32)....Fearing that the kingdom would return to the house of David if the people went to Jerusalem to worship, Jeroboam "made a house of high places" (v. 31).

A high place is an elevation, something lifted above the common level....In principle, every high place, every division, in Christianity today involves the uplifting, the exaltation, of something other than Christ. The things that are exalted may not be evil. On the contrary, they may be very good and may include even Bible study or Bible teaching.

What was written concerning Solomon and Jeroboam was written for our spiritual instruction today [cf. Rom. 15:4].

According to the Old Testament record, division is caused by lust and ambition. Solomon is an example of the former, and Jeroboam is an example of the latter.

The high places built by Solomon and Jeroboam seriously damaged the ground of oneness.

The ground of oneness is not simply a matter of one city, one church. The ground of oneness is deeper, richer, higher, and fuller than this. We all must learn that in this universe God has chosen only one place, and that place is the church. God requires us to go to this place He has chosen. Spiritually speaking, we must destroy every place other than the church and every name other than the name of Christ. This means that we must destroy our culture and religious background.... The places that we must destroy include our disposition, temperament, and habits. We must destroy everything that damages the oneness of the one new man. (*CWWL, 1979,* vol. 2, "The Genuine Ground of Oneness," pp. 314-316, 319, 288)

Further Reading: CWWL, 1979, vol. 2, "The Genuine Ground of Oneness," chs. 5, 8

*Enlightenment and inspiration:*_____

_____
_____
_____

Morning Nourishment

1 Cor. But of Him you are in Christ Jesus, who became
1:30 wisdom to us from God: both righteousness and
sanctification and redemption.

1 John In this you know the Spirit of God: Every spirit
4:2 which confesses that Jesus Christ has come in
the flesh is of God.

We should have nothing other than the person of Christ
and the unique way of the cross. Then we will enjoy Christ in
the church as the top portion of the rich produce of the land.
(*CWWL, 1979*, vol. 2, "The Genuine Ground of Oneness," p. 289)

Second John 7 says, "Many deceivers went out into the
world, those who do not confess Jesus Christ coming in the
flesh. This is the deceiver and the antichrist." The deceivers
mentioned here were heretics, like the Cerinthians, the false
prophets (1 John 4:1).

These deceivers do not confess Jesus Christ coming in the
flesh. This means that they do not confess that Jesus is God
incarnate. Thus, they deny the deity of Christ. Jesus was conceived of the Spirit (Matt. 1:18). To confess Jesus coming in
the flesh is to confess that, as the Son of God, He was divinely
conceived to be born in the flesh (Luke 1:31-35). The deceivers, the false prophets, would not make such a confession.

An antichrist is one who denies Christ's deity, denying that
Jesus is the Christ, that is, denying the Father and the Son by
denying that Jesus is the Son of God (1 John 2:22), not confessing that He has come in the flesh through the divine conception of the Holy Spirit (4:2-3). (*Life-study of 2 John*, p. 7)

Today's Reading

The Spirit works in the believers to confess to them that
Christ came in the flesh....According to 1 John 4:2, the dis-
cernment of spirits is based upon whether or not a spirit confesses that Jesus Christ has come in the flesh. Because the
spirit of a genuine prophet is motivated by the Holy Spirit of
truth, this spirit will confess the divine conception of Jesus
and affirm that He was born as the Son of God.

To deny that Jesus Christ has come in the flesh is to deny His divine conception, His incarnation, His birth, His humanity, His human living, and also His redemption. The New Testament makes it emphatically clear that Christ's redemption was accomplished in His human body and by the shedding of His blood.

Anyone who rejects Christ's incarnation and thereby rejects His redemption also denies Christ's resurrection. If Christ had never passed through death, it would not have been possible for Him to enter into resurrection.

If anyone denies Christ's incarnation, that one denies Christ's holy birth, humanity, human living, redemption through crucifixion, and resurrection. This utterly annuls the enjoyment of the genuine Trinity. In the light of this we see the crucial importance of the Spirit's work in the believers to confess that Jesus Christ has come in the flesh.

In 2 John 10 John…says, "If anyone comes to you and does not bring this teaching, do not receive him into your house, and do not say to him, Rejoice!" The pronoun *him* refers to a heretic, an antichrist, a false prophet, who denies the divine conception and deity of Christ, as today's modernists do. Such a one we must reject, not receiving him into our house or greeting him. Thus, we shall not have any contact with him or share in his heresy, heresy that is blasphemous to God and contagious like leprosy.

Just as bringing to others the divine truth of the wonderful Christ is an excellent deed (Rom. 10:15), so spreading the satanic heresy, which defiles the glorious divinity of Christ, is an evil work [cf. 2 John 11]. It is a blasphemy and abomination to God, and it is also a damage and curse to men. No believer in Christ and child of God should have any share in this evil. Even to greet such an evil one is prohibited. A severe and clear separation from this evil should be maintained. (*The Conclusion of the New Testament*, pp. 995-997, 2394)

Further Reading: Life-study of 2 John, msg. 2; The Conclusion of the New Testament, msgs. 93, 224

Enlightenment and inspiration:_____

_____

_____

_____

Morning Nourishment

Jude   Beloved, while using all diligence to write to
3   you concerning our common salvation, I...ex-
       hort *you* to earnestly contend for the faith once
       for all delivered to the saints.
20-21 But you, beloved, building up yourselves upon
       your most holy faith, praying in the Holy Spirit,
       keep yourselves in the love of God, awaiting the
       mercy of our Lord Jesus Christ unto eternal life.

["The faith" in Jude 3 is] not subjective faith as our believing but objective faith as our belief, referring to the things
we believe in, the contents of the New Testament as our faith
(Acts 6:7; 1 Tim. 1:19; 3:9; 4:1; 5:8; 6:10, 21; 2 Tim. 3:8; 4:7;
Titus 1:13), in which we believe for our common salvation.
This faith, not any doctrine, has been delivered once for all to
the saints. For this faith we should earnestly contend (1 Tim.
6:12). (Jude 3, footnote 3)

Today's Reading

We believe that the Bible, word by word, is divinely inspired
by God (2 Pet. 1:21), as the breath of God (2 Tim. 3:16)....We
must believe that the Bible is God's infallible Word.

God is uniquely one but triune, the Father, the Son, and
the Spirit (Matt. 3:16-17; 28:19; 2 Cor. 13:14; Eph. 2:18; 3:14-17;
Rev. 1:4-5). The Godhead is distinctively three, but They are
not three Gods separately. In the Old Testament and in the
New Testament, the Bible tells us definitely that God is one
(Deut. 4:35, 39; Psa. 86:10; 1 Cor. 8:4; 1 Tim. 2:5).

Christ was the very God in eternity (John 1:1) and became
a man in time (v. 14). His deity is complete, and His humanity
is perfect. Hence, He is both God and man (20:28; Rom. 9:5;
John 19:5; 1 Tim. 2:5), possessing both divinity and humanity.

Christ first became a man in incarnation (John 1:14) and
died on the cross for our redemption (1 Pet. 2:24; Rev. 5:9).
Then He rose from the dead for our regeneration (1 Pet. 1:3),
ascended to the heavens to be the Lord of all (Acts 2:33, 36;
10:36), and will come back as the Bridegroom to the church

(John 3:29; Rev. 19:7) and the King of kings to all the nations
(v. 16). These are the main aspects of the work of Christ.

A sinner must repent to God (Acts 2:38; 26:20) and believe in Christ (John 3:16; Acts 16:31) for forgiveness of sins
(10:43), for redemption (Rom. 3:24), for justification (Acts
13:39), and for regeneration (John 3:6) in order that he may
have the eternal life (v. 36) to become a child of God (1:12)
and a member of Christ (1 Cor. 12:27). This is our salvation
by God through faith (Eph. 2:4-9).

The church, composed of all the genuine believers in Christ,
as the Body of Christ (1:22-23; Col. 1:24), is universally one
(Eph. 4:4), and a local church as the expression of the Body
of Christ is locally one—one city, one church (Rev. 1:11).

[The above items] are the six main items of the proper
Christian faith. All real Christians do not have any disputa-
tions about these items....As the Body of Christ, the church
is universally one; as the expression of the Body of Christ, a
local church is locally one. This does not mean, however, that
a real believer in Christ who does not agree with one city, one
church is not saved. He or she is saved, but there is something lacking, not for salvation but for the proper church life.

The faith is the speciality of the church life....Concerning
these points of our Christian faith there should be no argu-
ment....There is no need for us to fight for other things. We
have to fight the good fight of such a faith (1 Tim. 6:12). We
have to contend for such a faith (Jude 3). We have to teach and
preach such a faith. (*CWWL, 1971,* vol 3, "The Speciality, Generality, and Practicality of the Church Life," pp. 416, 418-419)

The entire Blessed Trinity is employed and enjoyed by the
believers by their praying in the Holy Spirit, keeping themselves in the love of God, and awaiting the mercy of our Lord
unto eternal life. (*Life-study of Jude,* p. 21)

Further Reading: Life-study of Jude, msgs. 1-3; *CWWL, 1971,*
   vol 3, "The Speciality, Generality, and Practicality of the
   Church Life," ch. 1

*Enlightenment and inspiration:*_____
_____
_____
_____

Hymns, #981

1 In His Christ to head up all things
   Is our God's economy;
  Taking Christ as Head and center,
   All is one in harmony.

2 Christ as Head will be the center;
   God within will be the light.
  Christ enthroned, with God, His
     substance,
  Will fulfill His heart's delight.

3 Christ as life will be the content,
   Heading up all things in light;
  All the saints will be the vessel,
   To express His glory bright.

4 Satan hath himself injected
   Into man all things to spoil,
  Bringing darkness and corruption,
   God's eternal plan to foil.

5 Christ has come, Himself imparting
   Into man as life to save,
  That the pow'r of death and darkness
   May no more all things enslave.

6 Through the church, which is His Body,
   Christ as Head will sum up all;
  All will fitly join together,
   All things either great or small.

7 Under Christ, by His full headship,
   All in union will subsist;
  In the light the church expresses
   All in oneness will exist.

8 Owning Christ as Head and center,
   All will be in harmony;
  Through the shining of His Body
   All will share His liberty.

9   No more darkness and corruption,
     No more death and vanity;
     All will be released from bondage
     Throughout all eternity.

*Composition for prophecy with main point and sub-points:*_____

_____

_____

_____

_____

_____

_____

_____

_____

_____

_____

_____

_____

_____

_____

_____

_____

_____

_____

_____

_____

_____

_____

_____

_____

_____

_____

_____

_____

_____

_____

_____

_____

Aspects of the Church Life
under the Government of God

Scripture Reading: Deut. 1:9-18; 15:10; 22:9; 25:13-16; 1 Cor. 10:6, 11

Day 1

I. **The history of the children of Israel is a type of the church—1 Cor. 10:6, 11:**
   A. In His administrative arrangement God chose the children of Israel, the descendants of Abraham, and made them His people as a type of the church—Rom. 9:11-13; Acts 7:38:
      1. In the Old Testament the church is not mentioned in plain words, but there are types that portray the church—Gen. 2:21-24; 1 Chron. 28:11-19.
      2. The children of Israel, as the chosen people of God, are the greatest collective type of the church, in which we see that the church is chosen and redeemed by God, enjoys Christ and the Spirit as the life supply, builds God's habitation, inherits Christ as its portion, degrades and is captured, is recovered, and awaits Christ's coming.
      3. Paul applies the history of the children of Israel to the New Testament church life—1 Cor. 5:7-8; 10:1-13:
         a. In Hebrews and 1 Corinthians Paul points out clearly that what happened to the children of Israel is a type of the believers—10:6.
         b. The entire history of Israel is a story of the church.
   B. The Bible contains two histories—the history of Israel and the history of the church—Acts 7:1-53; Rev. 2—3:
      1. The history of the children of Israel is a type, and the history of the church is the fulfillment of the type.

2. In the Old Testament we have a type, a picture, of God's economy concerning the church, and in the New Testament God's economy concerning the church is fulfilled—1 Tim. 1:4; Eph. 1:10; 3:9-11.

Day 2 & Day 3

II. **God has a government in the universe, and there is also a government in the church—Rev. 4:2; 5:6; Acts 14:23; Titus 1:5:**
   A. God desires to execute His government in the universe through the church—Eph. 1:10, 22-23.
   B. Among the children of Israel there was a situation full of God's government and administration; the coordination and building in Exodus and Numbers were under God's administration and government.
   C. The divine government among God's people is a theocracy—Rev. 4:2; 5:6:
      1. Theocracy is government by God according to what He is—Psa. 89:14.
      2. God's administration among the children of Israel was a theocracy, meaning that God Himself came to govern, to rule, to administrate, the people directly yet through some agents; the agents were the priests and the elders working together for God's theocracy—Deut. 1:9-18.
      3. The theocracy among the children of Israel was a government according to God's constant speaking, as written in the law, and God's instant speaking, through the breastplate of the high priest by means of the Urim and the Thummim—Exo. 28:30; Lev. 8:8; Num. 27:21; Deut. 33:8.
   D. God's government in the administration of the church is neither autocracy nor democracy; autocracy is a kind of dictatorship, and democracy is government by the people according to the opinion of the people—Acts 14:23; Titus 1:5:

1. In the church life we honor God's authority as our government; thus, the government in the church is a theocracy—Eph. 1:10, 22-23; Col. 2:19.
2. Today God's rule is based on the Bible outside of us and on the Holy Spirit within us—2 Tim. 3:16-17; Rom. 8:5, 14.
3. When the elders follow the Holy Spirit in discussing matters, there is neither an autocracy nor a democracy but a theocracy, the rule of God.

Day 4

E. A proper king among the children of Israel was one who was instructed, governed, ruled, and controlled by the word of God—Deut. 17:14-20:
   1. The principle should be the same in the churches today—Acts 13:1-4a.
   2. In order to administrate the church, the elders must be constituted with the word of God—Col. 3:16:
      a. As a result, they will be under God's government, under God's rule and control.
      b. Spontaneously, God will be in their decisions, and the elders will represent God to manage the affairs of the church; this kind of management is theocracy.

III. **God's word spoken through Moses describes aspects of the church life under the government of God—Deut. 1:1:**
   A. In exercising His government, God required the children of Israel to worship Him in the unique place—Jerusalem—the worship center chosen by Him; they did not have the right to select a place according to their concept—12:1-12:
      1. Only the place where God put His name could be the worship center of His people—v. 5.
      2. God's people were to come to Mount Zion, the unique place chosen by God for corporate worship.

    3. God chose the unique place of worship for the purpose of keeping the oneness of His people— Psa. 133:1.

B. God takes care of the needs of all those who are part of His expression—Deut. 12:19; 14:27-29:
    1. In New Testament terms, this means that Christ takes care of every member of His Body—1 Cor. 12:14-27; Phil. 4:14-20.
    2. In the church life we should love the Lord Jesus, love His Body, and take care of the needs of all the members—2 Cor. 8:1-15.
C. If God's people would give to the poor, God would bless them in all their work and in all their undertakings—Deut. 15:10:
    1. In the church life today we should be happy when giving to the poor, knowing that God will bless us—2 Cor. 9:1-12.
    2. The dealing with mammon and the offering of material possessions are related to God's administration among the churches in resurrection—1 Cor. 16:1-3:
        a. The fact that material things are offered on the first day of the week indicates that they should be offered in resurrection, not in our natural life—vv. 1-2; Matt. 6:1-4.
        b. If we know resurrection life and the resurrection power, we will overcome money and material possessions, and what we have will be used for God's administration among the churches—1 Cor. 16:1-2; Acts 2:44-45; 4:32-35; Rom. 15:26.

D. Deuteronomy 25:13-16 is the ordinance concerning differing weights and measures:
    1. The dishonest practice of having differing weights and measures is a lie and is surely from Satan—John 8:44.

2. In spiritual application, to condemn a certain thing in others while justifying the same thing in ourselves indicates that we have different weights and measures, that is, different scales— one scale for measuring others and a different scale for measuring ourselves.

3. In the house of God, the church (1 Tim. 3:15), only one scale should be used to weigh everyone.

4. If we have only one scale, we will be fair, righteous, and just, even as God is, and we will keep the oneness and one accord in the church— Matt. 7:1-5.

E. The prohibition against sowing two kinds of seed in one's vineyard may typify the prohibition against teaching differently in the church—Deut. 22:9; 1 Tim. 1:3-4; 6:3; cf. Luke 8:11:

1. The church is God's vineyard, and in this vineyard only one kind of seed, one kind of teaching, should be sown—1 Cor. 3:9b; Acts 2:42.

2. If we teach differently, sowing more than one kind of seed, the "produce" in the church will be forfeited.

3. The apostles taught the same thing to all the saints in all the places and in all the churches— 1 Cor. 4:17; 7:17; 11:16; 14:33b-34:

   a. We also must teach the same thing in all the churches in every country throughout the earth—Matt. 28:19-20.

   b. There is no thought in the New Testament that a teaching is good for one church but not for the other churches; rather, the New Testament reveals that all the churches were the same in receiving the teachings—Titus 1:9.

F. Only by faith can we live the church life under the government of God—Eph. 1:22-23; 4:15; Col. 2:19; Gal. 2:16; 3:2, 5-9, 14:

1. God wants His people to do whatever He requires

not by self-effort but by faith—Heb. 10:39—11:1,
6, 9-12; 12:2; 1 Pet. 1:7-8.

2. God's economy is in faith, and faith is the unique
way for God to carry out His economy—1 Tim.
1:4; Gal. 2:20; 2 Cor. 5:7; 4:13.

3. The church is "the household of the faith"—
Gal. 6:10:

   a. The household of the faith is composed of all
   who are sons of God through faith in Christ
   Jesus—3:26.

   b. All the believers in Christ together consti-
   tute a universal household, the great family
   of God—a family that believes in God—6:10;
   Heb. 11:6.

Morning Nourishment

1 Cor. For I do not want you to be ignorant, brothers,
10:1 that all our fathers were under the cloud, and
all passed through the sea.

6 Now these things occurred as examples to us,
that we should not be ones who lust after evil
things, even as they also lusted.

In His old administrative arrangement God chose the children of Israel, the descendants of Abraham, and made them His people as a type of the church (Rom. 9:11-13; Acts 7:38). In the Old Testament the church is not mentioned in plain words. However, there are types that portray the church. The children of Israel, as the chosen people of God, are the greatest, collective type of the church, in which we can see that the church is chosen and redeemed by God, enjoys Christ and the Spirit as the life supply, builds God's habitation, inherits Christ as its portion, degrades and is captured, is recovered, and awaits Christ's coming. (*The Conclusion of the New Testament*, p. 156)

Today's Reading

In Hebrews and 1 Corinthians Paul points out clearly that what happened to the children of Israel is a type of us (1 Cor. 10:6). The entire history of Israel is a story of the church. The Bible, then, contains two histories—the history of Israel and the history of the church. The history of the children of Israel is a type, and the history of the church is the fulfillment of the type. Thus, the entire Bible gives us one revelation, the revelation of God's economy concerning the church. In the Old Testament we have a type, a picture, of God's economy concerning the church, whereas in the New Testament God's economy concerning the church is fulfilled. (*The Conclusion of the New Testament*, p. 156)

Before the New Testament age, that is, before the Lord's incarnation, God had chosen a people on this earth called Israel....Their forefather was Abraham. Then by Moses' time, at their exodus from Egypt, they became a race that had at least two million people. Since then, they have become a type of the church as God's elect in the New Testament. Thus, the Old Testament has a people, and the New Testament has a people....These two peoples are a description of one thing that God has done, and this one thing is the accomplishment of God's economy. Before God came to accomplish this economy, He first put out a type, a figure, a shadow. In God's economy the people of Israel are just a type, a figure, a shadow.

Some verses from the New Testament...show that the people of Israel are a type of the church. In 1 Corinthians 5 Paul says, "Our Passover, Christ, also has been sacrificed" (v. 7b). After the descendants of Abraham became a people, they eventually fell into the hand of Egypt and its king, Pharaoh. Pharaoh typifies Satan, and Egypt typifies the world. This means that God's chosen people fell into the hand of Satan and Satan's world, so there was the need of God's salvation to save them.

God exercised His salvation to save Israel out of Pharaoh's hand, out of Egypt, and bring them into the wilderness. In the wilderness God came to be a "tabernacle," indicating how He would come to dwell with His people to save them further and further so that they might become God in life and nature but not in the Godhead.

At the end of the New Testament, the Lord Jesus called the degraded church...the great Babylon, the mystery (Rev. 17:5). Eventually, the outcome of the church is the same as that of Israel. Israel's outcome was to be captured to Babylon....In Revelation 17 the Lord called the degraded church the great harlot, the great Babylon, and the mother of harlots (vv. 1, 5). This shows that the church is a fulfillment of the type of Israel. (*CWWL, 1994-1997,* vol. 1, "Living a Life according to the High Peak of God's Revelation," pp. 179-181)

Further Reading: Life-study of 1 Corinthians, msgs. 47-48;
  Truth Lessons—Level Three, vol. 2, lsn. 29; *CWWL, 1982,*
  vol. 1, "Experiencing Christ as the Offerings for the Church
  Meetings," ch. 3

*Enlightenment and inspiration:*_____

_____

_____

Morning Nourishment

Rev. Immediately I was in spirit; and behold, there
4:2 was a throne set in heaven, and upon the throne
there was One sitting.

5:6 And I saw in the midst of the throne and of the
four living creatures and in the midst of the elders
a Lamb standing as having *just* been slain, having seven horns and seven eyes, which are the
seven Spirits of God sent forth into all the earth.

Because the church has been degraded, whenever the word
government or *administration* is mentioned, some begin to
wonder immediately if this is Roman Catholicism. For this
reason, among most Protestant Christians, and particularly
among the more spiritual ones, there is a common concept
that it is better to have no government and no administration
than to have one. To them, as long as you understand that
the church is the Body of Christ and the house of God, it is
good enough....As long as others are helped to have the life
of God and to walk before the Lord, everything is all right.
To them, there is no need to have anything like government.
But, brothers and sisters, we are not more wise than God. In
the universe there is such a thing as the government of God
and the administration of God. This is something ordained
by God, and we cannot neglect it. (*CWWL, 1960,* vol. 2, "The
Elders' Management of the Church," pp. 134-135)

Today's Reading

In the Bible the kingdom is a matter of government. The
kingdom of God is the government of God. It is also the administration of God. Today the universe is in disorder because
God's government has not been honored. The elders should
not only see that in the universe there is God's salvation, God's
church, and God's house; they must further see that in the
universe there is God's government and God's administration. God is not a God of confusion. He is not a God without
principle and rule. God is a God with principles, rules, order,

and discipline. For this reason God must establish His administration and government in the universe.

Every book of the Bible shows God's government and administration. Consider the story of the Israelites leaving Egypt to pass through the wilderness to enter Canaan. Whether in the book of Exodus or in Numbers, we can see a very tightly knit coordination and building. This coordination and building is fully under God's government and administration. Among the Israelites, there was a situation full of God's government and administration. God did not let one thing get by loosely.... Everything great or small was under God's government and administration. Even minute details concerning the manner in which to wash themselves, the way to wash their clothes, and the way to shave their beards were not left to the choice of the Israelites. This was the Old Testament. Does this mean then that in the church God has no more government and administration? This cannot be true. In the New Testament every aspect of God's dealing with the church is under His government and administration. When the New Testament mentions the church, on the one hand, there are words full of life and the Spirit. On the other hand, there are also words full of government and administration.

In order to manage a church properly, an elder has to know that God desires to execute His government in the universe through the church. The church is definitely not a place without government and administration....You can read about the government of the church in the book of Romans. You can also read about the government of the church in the Epistles to the Corinthians. You can even read about the government of the church in Ephesians, 1 and 2 Timothy, and Titus. There is hardly a book among the New Testament Epistles that does not touch the government of the church. (*CWWL, 1960,* vol. 2, "The Elders' Management of the Church," pp. 135-136)

Further Reading: CWWL, 1960, vol. 2, "The Elders' Management of the Church," ch. 1

Enlightenment and inspiration:_____

_____

_____

_____

Morning Nourishment

Deut. You shall appoint for yourself judges and offi-
16:18 cers in all your cities which Jehovah your God
       is giving you, according to your tribes; and they
       shall judge the people with righteous judgment.
 33:8 And concerning Levi he said, May Your Thum-
       mim and Urim be with Your faithful man...

The portions of Deuteronomy which deal with the divine government are the word of God, not merely the word of Moses [Deut. 16:18-20; 17:8-20; 19:15-21; 21:1-9, 18-23; 22:13-30; 24:1-4, 7, 16; 25:1-3, 5-16]. We need to study all these portions in order to know God's mind and to know what He is thinking. God knows man and man's need, condition, and situation. Therefore, whatever God speaks regarding man is the final word.

The divine government among God's people is neither autocracy nor democracy but theocracy. Theocracy is government by God according to what He is. In the church life today, we exercise neither autocracy, which is a kind of dictatorship, nor democracy, which is according to the opinion of the people. Instead, we honor God's authority as our government, and thus the government in the church is a theocracy. (*Life-study of Deuteronomy*, p. 117)

Today's Reading

[Complicated cases were] investigated mainly by the priest [Deut. 17:8-9]. First, the priest investigated the case by going to God and staying with God. Second, in the presence of God, the priest would consider God's holy word. Third, as 33:8 indicates, the Levitical priests had the breastplate with the Urim and Thummim, which provided instant enlightenment.... Eventually, through the presence of God, the word of God, and the Urim and Thummim, the priest would gain a clear understanding of the divine judgment and then pass on this judgment to the presiding judge. The judge would then make a judgment according to what the priest had received from God and passed on to him. The judgment of the case, therefore, came through man, but it was of God and according to God. It was truly a matter of theocracy.

The government in the church should be neither autocratic nor democratic but theocratic.... All the saints are priests, but the elders are the leading priests. As such priests, they should stay in the Lord's presence with God's holy word and with today's breastplate—the mingled spirit with Christ and the church. As they remain in the Lord's presence with the word and the mingled spirit for the church, they will receive an understanding that is according to the Lord's thought, and this will become a decision as a kind of judgment. The elders should then administrate according to this divine judgment. Thus the elders function first as the leading priests and then as the administrators. (*Life-study of Deuteronomy,* p. 119)

Among the children of Israel in the Old Testament God governed His people according to His constant speaking, as written in the law, and His instant speaking, as revealed either through the breastplate of the high priest by means of the Urim and Thummim or through the prophets by the Spirit of God coming upon certain ones to enable them to speak God's word.... Moreover, God's government was executed through some human agents: the priests and the elders, the judges, or the kings as direct administrators, who worked together for God's theocracy. In the church in the New Testament the teaching of the apostles (Acts 2:42) replaces the law in God's administration, and the elders of the churches (Acts 14:23; Titus 1:5) are the direct administrators, who administrate according to the teaching of the apostles (1 Tim. 3:2; 5:17). In relation to the instant speaking of the Lord, all the believers in Christ, including the elders, are priests to God (1 Pet. 2:5; Rev. 1:6), having Christ as the High Priest living within them (Heb. 8:1; Rom. 8:10) and having the Holy Spirit mingled with their regenerated human spirit (Rom. 8:16) to replace the function of the Urim and Thummim. (Deut. 16:18, footnote 1)

Further Reading: Life-study of Deuteronomy, msg. 17

*Enlightenment and inspiration:*_____
_____
_____
_____

Morning Nourishment

Deut.   And when he sits on the throne of his king-
17:18-19 dom, he shall write out for himself a copy of
this law in a book, out of *that which is* before
the Levitical priests. And it shall be with him,
and he shall read in it all the days of his life,
in order that he may learn to fear Jehovah his
God by keeping all the words of this law and
these statutes and doing them.

Deuteronomy 17:14-20 speaks regarding the setting of a
king over the people....[God] Himself is the King; therefore,
for His people to want a king means that they want someone
to replace God. But God as our King should not be replaced and
cannot be replaced....The people wanted a king, even though
this was offensive to God (1 Sam. 8:4-22). Because of their in-
sistence, God gave them a king—Saul. Saul was not a good
king, for he was not a king who was according to God's heart.
Later God exercised His own choice and raised up David to
replace Saul. David was a king not according to God's preference but according to God's heart (1 Sam. 13:14). In the
sight of God David was the most pleasant king.

The king was to write out for himself a copy of the law
in a book, out of that which was before the Levitical priests
(Deut. 17:18). The law here refers to the Pentateuch. The king
was then to read in this copy of the law all the days of his
life in order that he might learn to fear Jehovah his God by
keeping all the words of the law (v. 19). This indicates that in
ruling over the people, he first had to be ruled himself by the
word of God. A proper king among the children of Israel was
one who was instructed, governed, ruled, and controlled by
the word of God. (*Life-study of Deuteronomy*, pp. 120-121)

Today's Reading

The principle should be the same with the elders in the
churches today. If the elders do not read the Bible and are
not controlled by the word of God, they cannot administrate
the church. In order to administrate, to manage, the church,

the elders must be reconstituted with the holy word of God.
As a result, they will be under God's government, under God's
rule and control. Then spontaneously God will be in their
decisions, and the elders will represent God to manage the
affairs of the church. This kind of management is theocracy.
(*Life-study of Deuteronomy,* p. 121)

In the place God had chosen, the children of Israel were
to eat before the Lord and rejoice (Deut. 12:7). Nowhere in the
book of Deuteronomy were God's people told that they should
go to the unique place to engage in mere "worship." Of course,
they were expected to worship the Lord in the place He had
chosen but not to worship according to their concept of what
worship is. Instead, they were to worship according to God's
thought, concept, of worship. According to the natural, human
concept, to worship is to kneel, to bow down, or to prostrate
ourselves before God. Even Muslims worship in such a way
in their mosques. Once I visited a Muslim mosque at the time
of worship. I noticed that among the worshippers there was
no sense of enjoyment. On the contrary, due to the lack of enjoyment, many of those worshippers looked older than their
years. The worship indicated in Deuteronomy 12 is not a matter of kneeling, bowing, or prostrating ourselves. According
to this chapter, to worship is to eat before the Lord. When they
came to the place God had chosen, God's people were to eat
the top portion of the offerings and sacrifices before God.

Have you ever thought that this is the kind of worship
God desires? In Deuteronomy 12 there is no mention of sing-
ing or even of praying. According to this portion of the Word,
proper worship is a matter of eating before God the rich produce of the good land. (*CWWL, 1979,* vol. 2, "The Genuine
Ground of Oneness," pp. 275-276)

Further Reading: Life-study of Deuteronomy, msg. 29; *CWWL,
1979,* vol. 2, "The Genuine Ground of Oneness," ch. 5;
CWWL, 1975-1976, vol. 3, "Young People's Training,"
chs. 12-13

*Enlightenment and inspiration:*_____

_____

_____

_____

Morning Nourishment

Deut. Be careful that you do not forsake the Levite all
12:19 your days upon the earth.
1 Cor. Now concerning the collection for the saints, just
16:1-2 as I directed the churches of Galatia, so you also
        do. On the first day of the week each one of you
        should lay aside in store to himself whatever he
        may have been prospered, that no collections be
        made when I come.

In Deuteronomy 13 we see that God takes care of Himself, and in Deuteronomy 12, that He takes care of His people as His expression. Now in the verses concerning aid to the needy [14:28—15:18] we see that God takes care of all those who are part of His expression.

The Levites, who had no job or other source of income but who lived on God, serving Him full time, were to be taken care of [12:19]....There was also to be provision for the sojourner, the orphan, and the widow [14:29]. Today we should also care for the needy ones among us....In the Lord's recovery, we need to care for the full-timers and the other needy ones.

In New Testament terms, this means that Christ takes care of every member of His Body. We all should follow this pattern. We should love the Lord Jesus, we should love His Body, and we should take care of the needs of all the members. In caring for the needs of the saints, it is best that we prepare for this by having a budget. This means that in a regular way we should lay something aside to use in taking care of needy saints. (*Life-study of Deuteronomy*, pp. 97, 96, 97)

Today's Reading

The people were required to open their hand to the poor one and to lend enough for his need in whatever he lacked (Deut. 15:8). Today we should not be reluctant to give to the poor brothers among us. When we give to meet the needs of the poor brothers, the Lord will return to us much more than we gave. All the believers who give willingly can testify of this.

"You must give to him, and your heart shall not be displeased when you give to him; for on account of this matter Jehovah your God will bless you in all your work and in all your undertakings" (v. 10)....We today should not be displeased when giving to the poor; instead, we should be happy, knowing that God will bless us and return much more to us. (*Life-study of Deuteronomy,* pp. 98-99)

All of fallen mankind are under the domination of mammon and material possessions (Matt. 6:19-21, 24-25, 30; 19:21-22; Luke 12:13-19). At the day of Pentecost, under the power of the Holy Spirit, all the believers overthrew this domination and had all their possessions in common for distribution to the needy ones (Acts 2:44-45; 4:32, 34-37). That practice, due to the weakness of the believers' fallen nature (see Acts 5:1-11; 6:1), did not last long. It was already over by the apostle Paul's time. Then the believers needed grace to overcome the power of mammon and material things and to release them from Satan's domination for an offering to the Lord to fulfill His purpose. Resurrection life is the supply for the believers to live such a life, a life trusting in God, not in treasures of material possessions, a life not for today but for the future, not for this age but for the coming age (Luke 12:16-21; 1 Tim. 6:17-19), a life that overthrows the usurpation of temporal and uncertain riches. This may be the reason that this dealing [in 1 Corinthians 16] follows the one concerning the reality of resurrection life [in chapter 15]. In any case this dealing is related to God's administration among the churches.

[In 1 Corinthians 16:2] "the first day of the week" is a symbol of the Lord's resurrection...[indicating that] our giving must be in resurrection life, not in our natural life....[This is] the victory in resurrection over your use of your money and material possessions. (*Life-study of 1 Corinthians,* pp. 625-626, 628)

Further Reading: Life-study of Deuteronomy, msgs. 14-15; *Life-study of 1 Corinthians,* msg. 69; *Life-study of 2 Corinthians,* msgs. 46-47, 49*

Enlightenment and inspiration:_____

_____

_____

Morning Nourishment

Deut. You shall not have in your bag differing weights.
25:13-15 ...You shall not have in your house differing
measures....A full and righteous weight...and
a full and righteous measure you shall have...
that your days may be extended upon the land
which Jehovah your God is giving you.

Gal. ...Let us do what is good toward all, but espe-
6:10 cially toward those of the household of the faith.

Deuteronomy 25:13-16 covers the judgment concerning
weights and measures. The children of Israel were not to
have in their bag differing weights, one heavy and one light,
nor were they to have in their house differing measures, one
large and one small (vv. 13-14).

To have differing weights and measures is a lie, and all
lies come from the enemy, Satan. The dishonest practice of
having differing weights and measures is surely from Satan.

The children of Israel were to have a full and righteous
weight and a full and righteous measure in order that their
days might be extended upon the God-given land (v. 15). Here
longevity is related to righteousness. Those who have lived
a long life often attribute their longevity to such matters as
taking care of their health, getting adequate sleep, and having a proper diet....In this verse living long upon the land
is clearly related to having full and righteous weights and
measures. (*Life-study of Deuteronomy*, p. 134)

Today's Reading

Those who have differing weights and measures actually
have differing scales. In the church life today, we may have
differing scales—one scale for measuring others and a different scale for measuring ourselves. Having differing scales, we
may condemn a certain thing in others but justify the same
thing in ourselves.

In the house of God, the church, there should be only one
scale....The same scale should be used to weigh everyone. If

we have only one scale, we will be fair, righteous, and just, even as God is. Because God is fair, righteous, and just, He measures everyone according to the same scale.

Although we should not have differing scales in the church life, one scale for weighing ourselves and other scales for weighing the brothers and sisters, we all have failed in this matter. Not one of us is an exception. Using the language of accounting, we may say that it is easy for us to "debit" others and "credit" ourselves. Instead of doing this, we should give others more credit and ourselves more debit.

Some saints who have the practice of using differing scales may move from one locality to another, hoping to find a more satisfactory church with more satisfactory elders. But because these saints have differing scales, no matter where they may go, they do not find the church and the elders to be satisfactory.

I emphasize the practice of having differing scales because this practice is a sickness, a disease, in the church life. This is the source of disaccord. Instead of keeping the oneness and the one accord, we have disaccord. May we all receive mercy from the Lord to no longer have differing scales but, like our God, to have the same scale for everyone. (*Life-study of Deuteronomy,* pp. 134-136)

For more than fifty years, I have been living by faith in the Lord. Often I have been very poor. Nevertheless, I can testify that even though I have been in extreme poverty, I never had any lack. I gathered little, but I had no lack. At other times I had an abundant supply, even large sums of money. However, I must testify that I did not have any excess. Therefore, I can testify from my experience that whenever I have gathered much, I have had no excess and that whenever I have gathered little, I have had no lack. Who balances the supply in this way? It is done by God with His heavenly balance. (*Life-study of 2 Corinthians,* p. 423)

Further Reading: Life-study of Deuteronomy, msg. 19; *Life-study of 2 Corinthians,* msg. 48

Enlightenment and inspiration:_____

_____

_____

Hymns, #947

1 God's kingdom today is a real exercise,
   But when Christ comes to reign, it will be a great prize;
   It is wisdom divine that we now may be trained
   That His plan be fulfilled and His justice maintained.

2 God's children, we're born to be kings with His Son,
   And we need to be trained that we may overcome
   And to know how to rule in His kingdom as kings,
   That His kingship thru us be expressed o'er all things.

3 Today we must learn to submit to His throne,
   How to have a strict life and His government own;
   His authority then we'll be able to share,
   O'er the nations to rule with God's Son as the Heir.

4 With a life strict to self we must righteousness hold,
   Kind to others in peace, and with God joyful, bold;
   In the kingdom's reality e'er to remain,
   For its manifestation prepared thus to reign.

5 Then Christ when He comes with the kingdom
      from God
   Will to us grant His kingship to share as reward;
   Thus the Lord will His righteousness through us
      maintain
   And His wisdom to heavenly powers make plain.

6 For this the apostle pressed on at all cost,
   For the kingdom assured that he would not be lost;
   'Tis for this he charged others, "Be true to the Lord,"
   That the kingdom might be unto them a reward.

7 O Lord, give us grace for Thy kingdom to live,
   To be trained that Thou may the reward to us give;
   Make the kingdom's reality our exercise,
   That its manifestation may be our great prize.

*Composition for prophecy with main point and
sub-points:*_____

Life and Blessing
under the Government of God

Scripture Reading: Deut. 30:15-20; Psa. 36:9a; 133:1, 3; Ezek. 34:26; Eph. 1:3

Day 1

I. In order to extend their days in the good land, the children of Israel were required to live under the government of God, doing all that God had commanded them through Moses—Deut. 30:15-20; 3:23-28; 4:1-24.

II. Moses set before the children of Israel life and death and charged them to choose life—30:15, 19-20:

A. With God is the fountain of life—Psa. 36:9a:

1. God wants us to take Him as the fountain, the source, of our life and our being—v. 9a.

2. The divine life may be considered the first and the basic attribute of God—Eph. 4:18; John 5:26; 1 John 5:11-12; Rom. 8:2:

a. According to the divine and eternal nature of the life of God, God's life is the unique life; only the life of God can be counted as life— John 1:4; 10:10b; 11:25; 14:6.

b. Life is the content of God and the flowing out of God; God's content is God's being, and God's flowing out is the impartation of Himself as life to us—Eph. 4:18; Rev. 22:1.

c. Life is the Triune God dispensed into us and living in us—Rom. 8:2, 6, 10-11.

Day 2

B. In Genesis 2:9, 16-17 we see two choices before man—the tree of life and the tree of the knowledge of good and evil:

1. The tree of life signifies the Triune God embodied in Christ as life to man in the form of food— v. 9; Rev. 2:7; John 1:4; 14:6a; 10:10b; 6:35, 57, 63.

2. The tree of the knowledge of good and evil signifies Satan as the source of death—Heb. 2:14.
3. The tree of life and the tree of the knowledge of
good and evil represent two principles of living—the principle of life (dependence on God)
and the principle of right and wrong (indepen-
dence from God)—Gen. 2:9, 16-17; 4:3-4; Jer. 17:5;
John 15:5.
4. These two trees are working within us as two
principles of living.
5. The Gospel of John reveals that the tree of life
is versus the tree of the knowledge of good and
evil—4:10-14, 20-21, 23-24; 9:1-3; 11:20-27.
6. In our Christian life and church life, we should
discern matters not according to right and wrong
but according to life and death—2 Cor. 11:3; Gen.
2:9, 16-17.

Day 3

C. By the resurrection life of Christ in our spirit, we
can be victorious over the attack of death upon the
church—Matt. 16:18; Acts 2:24; 2 Tim. 1:10:
1. Death is the characteristic of Satan's work; the
ultimate goal of his work is to saturate man with
death—Heb. 2:14-15.
2. Matthew 16:18 shows us from what source the
attack upon the church will come—"the gates
of Hades," that is, death:
a. Satan's special object is to spread death
within the church, and his greatest fear with
regard to the church is her resistance to his
power of death—Rev. 2:8, 10-11.
b. The church that is built upon "this rock"
can discern between death and life, and the
gates of Hades will not prevail against the
church—Matt. 16:18.
3. If we would overcome the attack of death, we
need to know Christ as the First and the Last
and the living One—the One who became dead

and lived again and the One who has the keys
of death and of Hades—Rev. 1:17-18; 2:8.

III. **Moses set before the children of Israel blessing
     and curse—Deut. 30:19:**
  A. In Genesis 1:26-28 God blessed man to be fruitful,
     multiply, fill the earth, and subdue it, because God
     saw on earth a living creature bearing His image
     and having His dominion.
  B. In order to be a blessing to His chosen people, God
     must have a kingdom, a realm, a sphere, on earth to
     exercise His administration under His full, divine
     authority—Matt. 6:10; Col. 1:13:
     1. Without such a kingdom, God does not have a
        realm in which to accomplish His purpose.
     2. Once there is a kingdom, the kingdom becomes
        the realm, the sphere, for God to exercise Him-
        self to bless us—Rev. 11:15.
     3. We all want to receive blessing, but we may not
        realize that the blessing requires a sphere of
        God's authority, a sphere under God's adminis-
        tration.

  C. God "has blessed us with every spiritual blessing
     in the heavenlies in Christ"—Eph. 1:3:
     1. God has blessed us with His speaking; all the
        speaking in verses 4 through 14 is God's bless-
        ing.
     2. *Every* indicates the all-inclusiveness of God's
        blessings.
     3. *Spiritual* indicates the relationship of God's
        blessings to the Holy Spirit:
        a. All the blessings with which God has blessed
           us are related to the Holy Spirit.
        b. The Spirit of God is not only the channel but
           also the reality of God's blessings.

     c. God the Father, God the Son, and God the
Spirit are all related to the blessings bestowed upon us—vv. 4-14; 3:16-17; 4:4-6.

     d. God's blessing is mainly the dispensing of
the Triune God into us—2 Cor. 13:14.

4. *Heavenlies* indicates not only the heavenly place
but also the heavenly nature, state, characteristic, and atmosphere of the spiritual blessings
with which God has blessed us:

     a. These blessings are from the heavens, having
a heavenly nature, heavenly state, heavenly
characteristic, and heavenly atmosphere.

     b. The believers in Christ are enjoying on earth
these blessings, which are spiritual as well
as heavenly.

5. *In Christ* indicates that Christ is the virtue, the
instrument, and the sphere in which God has
blessed us:

     a. In Christ God has blessed us with every spir-
itual blessing in the heavenlies.

     b. We praise the Lord that we are in Christ, who
is the virtue, the instrument, the sphere, and
the channel in which we have been blessed.

6. Since the nature of these blessings is spiritual,
we need to exercise our spirit to realize, experience, and partake of them in our spirit—Rom.
8:4.

Day 6

D. God's blessing is intrinsically related to oneness—
Psa. 133:1, 3:

1. The unity spoken of in verse 1 is a picture of the
genuine oneness in the New Testament; this
oneness is the processed and consummated Triune God mingled with the believers in Christ—
John 17:21-23.

2. *There* in Psalm 133:3 refers to the oneness upon
which the Lord commands the blessing—life forever.

E. Through His shepherding in His recovery by life, the Lord brings us into the enjoyment of His blessing and causes us to become a source of blessing under the showers of blessing—Ezek. 34:23, 26-27a, 29; Zech. 10:1:
   1. First, we ourselves enjoy the Lord's blessing, and then the Lord will cause us to become a source of blessing to others so that they may be supplied—Ezek. 34:26.
   2. God will cause the showers of blessing to come down in season—Zech. 10:1.

F. The greatest blessing that we receive from the Lord is not what the Lord gives us; it is what the Lord makes us, what He enables us to become—Rev. 3:12:
   1. The Lord's promise in Revelation 3:12 is to make the overcomer a pillar in the temple of God:
      a. Becoming a pillar in the temple of God involves transformation and building—21:22; 2 Cor. 3:18; Eph. 2:21-22; 4:16.
      b. It is a great blessing for the Lord to transform us and build us into His temple; this involves our being, what we are in Christ—Col. 1:27-28.
   2. If we see this vision, we will realize that in the church life the Lord's intention is not to do something outside of us but to transform us into another kind of being for His corporate expression—Rev. 21:10-11.
   3. In the church life we should not expect outward blessings; rather, it is crucial for us to realize that the Lord's blessing is to transform us into precious material and then build us into His dwelling place—Eph. 2:21-22.

G. The normal life of a Christian is a life of blessing, and the normal work of a Christian is a work of blessing—Num. 6:23-27; Matt. 5:3-11; 24:46; John 20:29; Gal. 3:14; 2 Cor. 9:6; Rom. 15:29.

H. We must realize that in our work, in our Christian life, and in our church life, everything depends on the Lord's blessing—Eph. 1:3; Mal. 3:10.

I. We need to pray, "Lord, please give us a vision that we may see the meaning of Your blessing, and have mercy on us that, unhindered, we may be able to receive Your blessing."

Morning Nourishment

Deut. ...I have put before you today life and good....
30:15-16 *If you obey the commandments of Jehovah your*
God, which I am commanding you today, to
love Jehovah your God and walk in His ways
and keep His commandments and His statutes
and His ordinances, then you will live and multiply, and Jehovah your God will bless you in
the land which you are entering to possess.

The children of Israel not only enjoyed the oracle of God;
they were also saturated with the fatness of God's house
(Psa. 36:8). God's house refers to the temple, which was the
continuation and enlargement of the Tent of Meeting. In
Psalm 36:9 the psalmist goes on to say, "With You is the fountain of life; / In Your light we see light." This verse is also
related to the temple. Only in the temple could God's people
enjoy the fountain of life. Furthermore, it was in the temple
that they could see light in God's light. This is an...indication
that the essence of the oneness of God's children is life and
light. (*CWWL, 1979,* vol. 2, "The Genuine Ground of Oneness,"
p. 247)

According to God's economy, the one who trusts in God is
like a tree planted by water, signifying God as the fountain
of living waters (Jer. 17:7-8; 2:13a). The tree grows beside
the river by absorbing all the riches of the water into it. This
is a picture of God's dispensing. In order to receive the divine
dispensing, we as the trees must absorb God as the water.
(*Life-study of Jeremiah,* p. 111)

Today's Reading

Life (zoe) is eternal. *Eternal* means "immortal." First John
1:2 says, "The life was manifested, and we have seen and
testify and report to you the eternal life, which was with
the Father and was manifested to us." Then Psalm 90:2b
says, "Indeed from eternity to eternity, You are God." Strictly
speaking, all lives that are mortal are not life. The real life
is immortal and eternal, and this real life is God Himself

because God is from eternity to eternity. God is eternal, so only God Himself is the real life.

Life is God's content and God's flowing out. God's content is God's being, so life is God's inner being (Eph. 4:18a). God's flowing out is the impartation of Himself as life to us. In Revelation 22:1 we see the river of water of life flowing out from the throne of God. This is God's flowing out. Life is God's content, His inner being, and life is God flowing out into us and being imparted into our being.

Life is Christ (John 14:6a; Col. 3:4a; 1 John 5:12a). Christ is the embodiment of God, who is life. Colossians 2:9 says that all the fullness of the Godhead dwells in Christ bodily. God as life is embodied in Christ, and Christ is the expression of God. John 1:18 says that no one has ever seen God, but the only begotten Son has declared Him. Then Hebrews 1:3 shows that Christ is the effulgence of God's glory. This means that Christ is the expression of God, who is life.

Finally, we need to point out that life is the Holy Spirit. The Holy Spirit is the reality of Christ (John 14:16-17; 1 Cor. 15:45b). The Son is the embodiment of the Father, and the Spirit is the reality of the Son. Romans 8:2a uses the term *the Spirit of life,* and 2 Corinthians 3:6b says that the Spirit gives life. Thus, the Holy Spirit today is the Spirit of life who gives life to us. We must stress that the Spirit in the New Testament has two aspects. On the one hand, He is the Spirit of power; on the other hand, He is the Spirit of life.

Life is the Triune God dispensed into us and living in us. The Father is the source, the Son is the course, and the Spirit is the flow. The Triune God is dispensed into us in His Divine Trinity and is now living within us. (*CWWL, 1979,* vol. 1, "Basic Lessons on Life," pp. 517-518)

Further Reading: Life-study of Deuteronomy, msgs. 1-4; *CWWL, 1979,* vol. 2, "The Genuine Ground of Oneness," ch. 2; *Life-study of Jeremiah,* msg. 16; *CWWN,* vol. 37, ch. 2

Enlightenment and inspiration:_____

_____

_____

Morning Nourishment

Deut. ...I have set before you life and death, blessing
30:19-20 and curse; therefore choose life that you and
your seed may live, in loving Jehovah your
God by listening to His voice and holding fast
to Him; for He is your life and the length of
your days, that you may dwell upon the land
which Jehovah swore to your fathers...

God wanted man to depend on Him for his living in the
same way that he was dependent upon food for his living. "For
in Him we live and move and are" (Acts 17:28). Thus, God uses
two trees to speak to us in a parable. The tree of life and the
tree of the knowledge of good and evil are a kind of parable.
They show us that man has two different kinds of food and can
live either by life or by the knowledge of good and evil, that is,
the knowledge of right and wrong....The two trees were put
there to show us that man, especially a Christian, can live on
earth according to two different principles. Man can live according to the principle of right and wrong or according to the
principle of life. Some Christians take the principle of right
and wrong as the standard for their living, while other Christians take the principle of life as their standard for living.
(Watchman Nee, *Two Principles of Living* (booklet), pp. 2-3)

Today's Reading

[We need] to see these two principles for living. What does
it mean when a person lives according to right and wrong?
What does it mean when a person lives according to life? Many
people only have the tree of the knowledge of good and evil
in their lives. Other people have the tree of life in their lives.
Some have both trees. The Word of God tells us, however, that
he who eats of the tree of the knowledge of good and evil shall
surely die, while he who eats of the tree of life shall live.

If our conduct is controlled by the principle of right and
wrong, then we ask if something is right or wrong whenever
we have to make a decision. Would it be good to do this, or
would it be evil? When we ask whether it is good, we are, in

effect, asking ourselves, "Am I right to do this or not?" Many people consider much whether something is good or evil. They consider whether they can or cannot do a certain thing. They ask, "Is this right or wrong?" As they carefully consider a certain matter, being Christians, they determine whether it is good and right to do that thing. By taking care to decide whether or not something is good and right, they consider themselves to be good Christians.

God's Word says, "The tree of the knowledge of good and evil, of it you shall not eat; for in the day that you eat of it you shall surely die" (Gen. 2:17). At the most, this practice is only a discerning of good from evil. At best, it is merely choosing and rejecting—choosing good and rejecting evil. This is...the Old Testament, the law, worldly religions, human morality, and human ethics, but it is not Christianity.

Christianity is life,...not a matter of asking whether something is right or wrong...[but] of checking with the life inside us whenever we do something. What does the new life which God has given us tell us inwardly about this matter?...What does our inner life say? If the life is strong and active within us, we can do this; if the life is cold and retreating within us, we should not. Our principle for living is inward instead of outward.

The standard of Christian living does not only deal with evil things but also with good and right things. Many matters are right according to human standards, but the divine standard pronounces them wrong because they lack the divine life.... Decisions should be made according to God's life as it rises up or recedes within us....Do we feel joyful inwardly about this matter? Do we have spiritual happiness and peace? These are the matters that decide our spiritual path. (*Two Principles of Living* (booklet), pp. 2-3, 6-9, 13-15)

Further Reading: Life-study of Deuteronomy, msgs. 9, 24, 27, 30; *CWWN,* vol. 56, "Two Principles of Living," pp. 418-432; *The Conclusion of the New Testament,* msg. 265; *CWWL, 1994-1997,* vol. 3, "The God-man Living," ch. 14

*Enlightenment and inspiration:*_____
_____
_____
_____

Morning Nourishment

Matt. And I also say to you that you are Peter, and
16:18 upon this rock I will build My church, and the
gates of Hades shall not prevail against it.

Rev. And the living One; and I became dead, and be-
1:18 hold, I am living forever and ever; and I have
the keys of death and of Hades.

The riches of God are in Christ, and the riches of Christ
are manifested through the church....Since the church is the
testimony of the riches of God, its characteristics must be
the characteristics of Christ....The characteristics of Christ
are encapsulated in the words He said when He raised Laza-
rus from the dead, "I am the resurrection and the life" (John
11:25)....Since the church is the vessel of Christ on earth, it
should express this life and resurrection. God intends for the
church to manifest the life of Christ. Hence, the church must
be full of life.

The main goal of the Lord coming to earth is for man to
have life (John 10:10), that is, for man to receive God's life....
God's Christ is life, and God's Christ is resurrection, and the
church is the vessel of this life and resurrection. (*CWWN*,
vol. 44, pp. 881-882)

Today's Reading

Since God's goal today is the church, Satan's attacks are
directed specifically against the church. Satan does not neces-
sarily stumble Christians or the church with the enticement
of sin or the world, because these things are too obvious....The
ultimate weapon Satan uses to attack the church is death.
Death is not easily identifiable; it can creep secretly into the
church. This does not mean that Satan will not use the world
and sin to attack the church. It means that Satan can use refined and moral things, not just filthy and treacherous sins
to attack Christians. Many refined and moral things are filled
with death, and Satan can easily utilize these deadly things
to attack the church.

Matthew 16:18 says that the foundation of the Lord's

church is Christ the Rock, and the gates of Hades cannot prevail against this church. Hades is death....The only reason that death cannot prevail over the church is that the church is built upon Christ the Rock....If the church is built on Christ the Rock, it will distinguish between death and life, and the gates of Hades will not prevail against it.

Romans 8:10 is on the body and the spirit, while John 12 is on the soul, both the preserving and the losing of the soul.... Everything that issues from the body or from the soul results in death, which is Hades, whereas everything that issues from the spirit results in life. A man may be very talkative; he may be very wordy and may love to speak vain and improper words. A man also may be clear in logic and excellent in eloquence. All these things are but the products of the flesh, the soul, and the natural life. None of them is of the spirit or of Christ. Hence, there is no life; there is only death. A Christian should not ask whether a thing is good or evil but should ask from where a thing originates. Does it originate from the natural life, the flesh, the soul, or does it originate from the spirit? Of all the things that a Christian possesses, only those that originate from the spirit are of life, and only they can give others life. Nothing else—no matter how good, profitable, or nice— gives life.

The church does not need good doctrines, good theology, or wonderful expositions. The church needs life, the resurrection life of Christ. No doctrine, idea, theology, or exposition can replace the life of Christ. Only the life of Christ and that which issues from it will prevail against the gates of Hades. Everything else is just disguised forms of death and cannot withstand the attacks of Satan. May the Lord be merciful to us, and may He keep us from touching death or bringing death into the church. May God fill the church with life, and may Satan find no opening to attack the church. (*CWWN*, vol. 44, pp. 882-885)

Further Reading: CWWN, vol. 44, chs. 113-114

Enlightenment and inspiration:_____

_____

_____

Morning Nourishment

Deut.   **...I have set before you life and death, blessing**
30:19 **and curse; therefore choose life that you and**
      your seed may live.
Gen.   **And God blessed them; and God said to them,**
1:28 **Be fruitful and multiply, and fill the earth and**
      subdue it, and have dominion...

God blessed man to be fruitful, multiply, fill the earth, and conquer it (Gen. 1:28)....God is rich and God is rich in blessing, but before the creation of man there was no object to receive His blessing in full....According to the record of Genesis 1, God did not begin to bless until the time when the living creatures came into being (Gen. 1:22). Yet, only the human life is up to the standard to receive God's blessing in full. After God created man, He was able to see on earth a living creature bearing His image and having His dominion. Immediately God bestowed His full blessing upon man. (*Life-study of Genesis,* p. 105)

Today's Reading

If we are to receive God's blessing, we need to meet the qualifications..., [which] are image and dominion. If there is the image of God with God's dominion in your home, you can be assured that the blessing of God will be there....God's blessing always follows His expression and His representation.

God's blessing is always with the priesthood and the kingship....The priesthood is for God's image; the kingship is for God's dominion. As long as we exercise the priesthood to contact God, to behold God and to reflect the image of glory, we have the kingship. God's blessing follows immediately.

The blessing is fruit-bearing, increase, multiplication, and the filling of the earth....God...created a man in His image, giving him authority to have dominion for the Almighty on earth. This man was ready for God's blessing. God's blessing was to enable this man to be fruitful. One would become ten, ten would become one hundred, one hundred would become a thousand, a thousand would become a hundred thousand, a hundred thousand would become a million, and a million would become a billion, until the whole earth was filled with beautiful faces expressing God and representing God.

How much God is able to bless us depends on how much we express Him and represent Him. If we express Him and represent Him in an adequate way, we will surely have His full blessing in multiplication and fruit-bearing. (*Life-study of Genesis,* pp. 105-107)

We must see that the Lord withholds no good thing from us. If the work is not going well, if the brothers and sisters are in a poor condition, or if the number of saved ones is not increasing, we should not use the environment or certain people as an excuse. We cannot blame the brothers. I am afraid that the real reason lies with our harboring of some frustrations to the blessing. If the Lord can get through in us, the Lord's blessing will be greater than our capacity. Once God said to the Israelites, "Prove Me, if you will, by this,…whether I will open to you the windows of heaven and pour out blessing for you until there is no room for it" (Mal. 3:10). God is still saying this today. The normal life of a Christian is a life of blessing, and the normal work of a Christian is a work of blessing. If we do not receive blessing, we should say, "Lord, perhaps I am the problem." (*Expecting the Lord's Blessing* (booklet), pp. 7-8)

The principle of God's blessing is also seen in the case of Naomi in the book of Ruth.…Since Naomi was humbled and subdued under God's judging hand, God's blessing was brought in.…This case shows that God's heart is to bless, but man's questionable condition requires God's judging hand first.…Whoever is willing to judge and condemn himself under God's judging will meet grace and receive blessing. (*CWWL, 1957,* vol. 3, "The Living God and the God of Resurrection," pp. 46-47)

Further Reading: Life-study of Genesis, msg. 9; *CWWL, 1957,* vol. 3, "The Living God and the God of Resurrection," ch. 6; *CWWN,* vol. 56, "Expecting the Lord's Blessing," pp. 435-446

Enlightenment and inspiration:_____
_____
_____

Morning Nourishment

Eph. **Blessed be the God and Father of our Lord Jesus**
1:3 **Christ, who has blessed us with every spiritual**
blessing in the heavenlies in Christ.

Rom. **That the righteous requirement of the law might**
8:4 **be fulfilled in us, who do not walk according to**
the flesh but according to the spirit.

The praise in Ephesians 1:3 is deep and profound, en-
compassing the entire New Testament economy. Here we
have not only creation, indicated by the title *God,* but also
incarnation, indicated by the title *the God of our Lord Jesus
Christ.*...In the incarnation He is the Father to impart His
life to all His sons....The highest praise to God says that our
God the Creator became a man and that our God is also the
life-imparting Father....Whatever Christ has attained and
obtained is transmitted to the church.

The title *Our Lord Jesus Christ* is rich in meaning. *Lord*
signifies Christ's lordship, *Jesus* signifies His humanity to
be our Redeemer and Savior, and *Christ* signifies that He is
God's anointed One. This is a further indication that 1:3 is
the top praise, the highest well-speaking of God. We all need
to speak well concerning God in this way: in the way of creation, incarnation, impartation of life, and transmission, with
redemption, the Redeemer, the Savior, and the anointed One
to accomplish God's eternal purpose. (*Life-study of Ephesians,*
pp. 17-18)

Today's Reading

God has blessed us with His good, fine, and fair speakings. Every such speaking is a blessing to us. Ephesians 1:4
through 14 are an account of such speakings, such blessings.

The word *every* [in 1:3] indicates the all-inclusiveness of
God's blessings. It includes all, with no exception.

All these blessings are spiritual. This indicates the relationship of God's blessings to the Holy Spirit. Being spiritual,
all the blessings with which God has blessed us are related

to the Holy Spirit. The Spirit of God is not only the channel, but also the reality, of God's blessings. In this verse, God the Father, God the Son, and God the Spirit are all related to the blessings bestowed upon us....God's blessing is mainly the dispensation of the Triune God into us.

Heavenlies here indicates not only the heavenly place, but also the heavenly nature, state, characteristic, and atmosphere of the spiritual blessings with which God has blessed us. They are from the heavens with a heavenly nature, heavenly state, heavenly characteristic, and heavenly atmosphere. The believers in Christ are enjoying on earth these heavenly blessings. They are heavenly as well as spiritual....The blessings bestowed upon us are of God the Father, in God the Son, through God the Spirit, and in the heavenlies.

Finally, all these spiritual blessings are in Christ. Christ is the virtue, the instrument, and the sphere in which God has blessed us. Outside of Christ, without Christ, God has nothing to do with us. But in Christ He has blessed us with every spiritual blessing in the heavenlies.

If we are in ourselves, we are through with God's blessing. Hallelujah, we are in Christ, who is the sphere, the channel, the instrument, and the virtue in which we have been blessed! (*Life-study of Ephesians,* pp. 21-22)

If these blessings were physical, material blessings, they would need to be enjoyed and experienced by us in our physical body. Likewise, if they were psychological blessings, we could realize them by exercising our soul—our mind, emotion, and will. However, these are spiritual blessings, the blessings of the Holy Spirit. Since the nature of all these blessings is spiritual, we need to exercise our spirit to realize, enjoy, and partake of them in our spirit. (*CWWL, 1966,* vol. 2, "The Divine Spirit with the Human Spirit in the Epistles," p. 305)

Further Reading: Life-study of Ephesians, msg. 2; *CWWL, 1966,* vol. 2, "The Divine Spirit with the Human Spirit in the Epistles," ch. 7

Enlightenment and inspiration:_____

_____

_____

_____

Morning Nourishment

Psa. ...How good and how pleasant it is for brothers
133:1-3 to dwell in unity! It is like the fine oil upon the
head that ran down...; like the dew...that came
down upon the mountains of Zion. For there
Jehovah commanded the blessing: Life forever.

Ezek. ...I will make them...a blessing, and I will cause
34:26 the showers to come down in their season; there
will be showers of blessing.

Psalm 133 is the praise of a saint, in his going up to Zion, concerning Jehovah's commanded blessing on brothers who dwell in oneness. When Zion is built up and when God is resting there and dwelling in Jerusalem,...we have a place where we can gather and where we can dwell together in oneness. How good and how pleasant this is! (Psa. 133:1, footnote 1)

The eternal life of God (John 3:16; Eph. 4:18)...is commanded by God as a blessing to those who dwell together in oneness in the church life....Psalm 133 typifies the church living—the highest living, a living in which the brothers dwell together in oneness. Such a living causes God to come in to bless us with the anointing Spirit, the watering grace, and the eternal life. (Psa. 133:3, footnote 3)

Today's Reading

[In Ezekiel 34:26] the Lord promised not only that His people would receive His blessing but also that He would make them a blessing....First, we ourselves will enjoy the Lord's blessing, and then He will cause us to become a source of blessing to others so that they may be supplied.

The Lord promises that there will be "showers of blessing."...Many times in the meetings of the local churches we sense that something is not only flowing but also coming down like a shower. Sometimes even at home after the meeting, we have the sense that the showers of blessing are still coming down upon us. This is the strongest sign that the Lord's blessing is upon the local church. He sends us showers of blessing in season, so timely. (*Life-study of Ezekiel,* pp. 183-184)

The Lord's promise in Revelation 3:12 is not to give us something but to make us something. Whenever we think of the Lord's promises, we always think that He will give us something. According to our concept, a promise is related to a blessing. To us, without a blessing, there can be no promise. But in 3:12 the Lord did not say, "Him I will give"; He said, "Him I will make." In 3:12 the Lord does not promise to give us holiness or a heavenly blessing. No, here He promises to make us become something—a pillar in the temple of God.

Becoming a pillar in the temple of God involves two things—transformation and building. Since I came to this country, my burden has been on these two matters. The greatest blessing the Lord can render us is to transform us and to build us into His temple....[What does it mean] to be made a pillar in the temple of God?...Those who have reached the level of the church in Philadelphia have the proper understanding within them. If we are on this level, then we are ready for the Lord to transform us. If we use the little power we have received of the Lord on His word and mean business with Him, then we are ready to be transformed and are in the proper position for the Lord to make us a pillar. This requires that we firstly be transformed into precious material and secondly that we be built into a pillar. How can we, who are clay, become a pillar in God's temple? There is no way except to be transformed from clay into precious stone and then to be built into God's building....Revelation 2:17...indicates that we can be transformed into a white stone by eating Him as the hidden manna. This is truly the greatest blessing. This involves our very being, for it is related to what we are. The greatest blessing is not what the Lord gives us, but what the Lord makes us. (*Life-study of Revelation*, p. 370)

Further Reading: Life-study of the Psalms, msg. 42; Life-study of Jeremiah, msg. 20; CWWL, 1957, vol. 2, "The Administration of the Church and the Ministry of the Word," ch. 5

Enlightenment and inspiration:_____

_____

_____

Hymns, #546

1   I love my Lord, but with no love of mine,
     For I have none to give;
   I love Thee, Lord, but all the love is Thine,
     For by Thy love I live.
   I am as nothing, and rejoice to be
   Emptied, and lost, and swallowed up in Thee.

2   Thou, Lord, alone, art all Thy children need,
     And there is none beside;
   From Thee the streams of blessedness proceed,
     In Thee the bless'd abide.
   Fountain of life, and all-abounding grace,
   Our source, our center, and our dwelling place.

Hymns, #1191

1   From my spirit within flows a fountain of life—
     The Triune God flowing in me;
   God the Father's the source, Christ the Son is
       the course,
     And the Spirit imparts life to me.

     Lord, I treasure the sweet flow of life,
       And my soul-life at last I lay down;
     O Lord, deepen the pure flow of life;
       At Your coming may life be my crown.

2   In the tender, fresh grass Jesus makes me lie down;
     He leads me by waters of rest;
   No more struggle and strain; all self-effort is vain;
     In the flow I am perfectly blessed.

3   Jesus called me one day to the Holiest Place,
     To live in His presence divine;
   Hallelujah, I've heard an encouraging word:
     "Abide—you're a branch in the vine."

Composition for prophecy with main point and sub-points: 1 800-527-0656 To help rescue a child (6-5-20) MISSION RESCUE Life rescuelife.org Today on d Sereen

Opeyemi Neighbor Ib -0802-639-26 9

Reading Schedule for the Recovery Version of the Old Testament with Footnotes

Wk.	Lord's Day	Monday	Tuesday	Wednesday	Thursday	Friday	Saturday
1	Gen. 1:1-5 ☐	1:6-23 ☐	1:24-31 ☐	2:1-9 ☐	2:10-25 ☐	3:1-13 ☐	3:14-24 ☐
2	4:1-26 ☐	5:1-32 ☐	6:1-22 ☐	7:1—8:3 ☐	8:4-22 ☐	9:1-29 ☐	10:1-32 ☐
3	11:1-32 ☐	12:1-20 ☐	13:1-18 ☐	14:1-24 ☐	15:1-21 ☐	16:1-16 ☐	17:1-27 ☐
4	18:1-33 ☐	19:1-38 ☐	20:1-18 ☐	21:1-34 ☐	22:1-24 ☐	23:1—24:27 ☐	24:28-67 ☐
5	25:1-34 ☐	26:1-35 ☐	27:1-46 ☐	28:1-22 ☐	29:1-35 ☐	30:1-43 ☐	31:1-55 ☐
6	32:1-32 ☐	33:1—34:31 ☐	35:1-29 ☐	36:1-43 ☐	37:1-36 ☐	38:1—39:23 ☐	40:1—41:13 ☐
7	41:14-57 ☐	42:1-38 ☐	43:1-34 ☐	44:1-34 ☐	45:1-28 ☐	46:1-34 ☐	47:1-31 ☐
8	48:1-22 ☐	49:1-15 ☐	49:16-33 ☐	50:1-26 ☐	Exo. 1:1-22 ☐	2:1-25 ☐	3:1-22 ☐
9	4:1-31 ☐	5:1-23 ☐	6:1-30 ☐	7:1-25 ☐	8:1-32 ☐	9:1-35 ☐	10:1-29 ☐
10	11:1-10 ☐	12:1-14 ☐	12:15-36 ☐	12:37-51 ☐	13:1-22 ☐	14:1-31 ☐	15:1-27 ☐
11	16:1-36 ☐	17:1-16 ☐	18:1-27 ☐	19:1-25 ☐	20:1-26 ☐	21:1-36 ☐	22:1-31 ☐
12	23:1-33 ☐	24:1-18 ☐	25:1-22 ☐	25:23-40 ☐	26:1-14 ☐	26:15-37 ☐	27:1-21 ☐
13	28:1-21 ☐	28:22-43 ☐	29:1-21 ☐	29:22-46 ☐	30:1-10 ☐	30:11-38 ☐	31:1-17 ☐
14	31:18—32:35 ☐	33:1-23 ☐	34:1-35 ☐	35:1-35 ☐	36:1-38 ☐	37:1-29 ☐	38:1-31 ☐
15	39:1-43 ☐	40:1-38 ☐	Lev. 1:1-17 ☐	2:1-16 ☐	3:1-17 ☐	4:1-35 ☐	5:1-19 ☐
16	6:1-30 ☐	7:1-38 ☐	8:1-36 ☐	9:1-24 ☐	10:1-20 ☐	11:1-47 ☐	12:1-8 ☐
17	13:1-28 ☐	13:29-59 ☐	14:1-18 ☐	14:19-32 ☐	14:33-57 ☐	15:1-33 ☐	16:1-17 ☐
18	16:18-34 ☐	17:1-16 ☐	18:1-30 ☐	19:1-37 ☐	20:1-27 ☐	21:1-24 ☐	22:1-33 ☐
19	23:1-22 ☐	23:23-44 ☐	24:1-23 ☐	25:1-23 ☐	25:24-55 ☐	26:1-24 ☐	26:25-46 ☐
20	27:1-34 ☐	Num. 1:1-54 ☐	2:1-34 ☐	3:1-51 ☐	4:1-49 ☐	5:1-31 ☐	6:1-27 ☐
21	7:1-41 ☐	7:42-88 ☐	7:89—8:26 ☐	9:1-23 ☐	10:1-36 ☐	11:1-35 ☐	12:1—13:33 ☐
22	14:1-45 ☐	15:1-41 ☐	16:1-50 ☐	17:1—18:7 ☐	18:8-32 ☐	19:1-22 ☐	20:1-29 ☐
23	21:1-35 ☐	22:1-41 ☐	23:1-30 ☐	24:1-25 ☐	25:1-18 ☐	26:1-65 ☐	27:1-23 ☐
24	28:1-31 ☐	29:1-40 ☐	30:1—31:24 ☐	31:25-54 ☐	32:1-42 ☐	33:1-56 ☐	34:1-29 ☐
25	35:1-34 ☐	36:1-13 ☐	Deut. 1:1-46 ☐	2:1-37 ☐	3:1-29 ☐	4:1-49 ☐	5:1-33 ☐
26	6:1—7:26 ☐	8:1-20 ☐	9:1-29 ☐	10:1-22 ☐	11:1-32 ☐	12:1-32 ☐	13:1—14:21 ☐

Reading Schedule for the Recovery Version of the Old Testament with Footnotes

Wk.	Lord's Day	Monday	Tuesday	Wednesday	Thursday	Friday	Saturday
27	14:22—15:23 ☐	16:1-22 ☐	17:1—18:8 ☐	18:9—19:21 ☐	20:1—21:17 ☐	21:18—22:30 ☐	23:1-25 ☐
28	24:1-22 ☐	25:1-19 ☐	26:1-19 ☐	27:1-26 ☐	28:1-68 ☐	29:1-29 ☐	30:1—31:29 ☐
29	31:30—32:52 ☐	33:1-29 ☐	34:1-12 ☐	Josh. 1:1-18 ☐	2:1-24 ☐	3:1-17 ☐	4:1-24 ☐
30	5:1-15 ☐	6:1-27 ☐	7:1-26 ☐	8:1-35 ☐	9:1-27 ☐	10:1-43 ☐	11:1—12:24 ☐
31	13:1-33 ☐	14:1—15:63 ☐	16:1—18:28 ☐	19:1-51 ☐	20:1—21:45 ☐	22:1-34 ☐	23:1—24:33 ☐
32	Judg. 1:1-36 ☐	2:1-23 ☐	3:1-31 ☐	4:1-24 ☐	5:1-31 ☐	6:1-40 ☐	7:1-25 ☐
33	8:1-35 ☐	9:1-57 ☐	10:1—11:40 ☐	12:1—13:25 ☐	14:1—15:20 ☐	16:1-31 ☐	17:1—18:31 ☐
34	19:1-30 ☐	20:1-48 ☐	21:1-25 ☐	Ruth 1:1-22 ☐	2:1-23 ☐	3:1-18 ☐	4:1-22 ☐
35	1 Sam. 1:1-28 ☐	2:1-36 ☐	3:1—4:22 ☐	5:1—6:21 ☐	7:1—8:22 ☐	9:1-27 ☐	10:1—11:15 ☐
36	12:1—13:23 ☐	14:1-52 ☐	15:1-35 ☐	16:1-23 ☐	17:1-58 ☐	18:1-30 ☐	19:1-24 ☐
37	20:1-42 ☐	21:1—22:23 ☐	23:1—24:22 ☐	25:1-44 ☐	26:1-25 ☐	27:1—28:25 ☐	29:1—30:31 ☐
38	31:1-13 ☐	2 Sam. 1:1-27 ☐	2:1-32 ☐	3:1-39 ☐	4:1—5:25 ☐	6:1-23 ☐	7:1-29 ☐
39	8:1—9:13 ☐	10:1—11:27 ☐	12:1-31 ☐	13:1-39 ☐	14:1-33 ☐	15:1—16:23 ☐	17:1—18:33 ☐
40	19:1-43 ☐	20:1—21:22 ☐	22:1-51 ☐	23:1-39 ☐	24:1-25 ☐	1 Kings 1:1-19 ☐	1:20-53 ☐
41	2:1-46 ☐	3:1-28 ☐	4:1-34 ☐	5:1—6:38 ☐	7:1-22 ☐	7:23-51 ☐	8:1-36 ☐
42	8:37-66 ☐	9:1-28 ☐	10:1-29 ☐	11:1-43 ☐	12:1-33 ☐	13:1-34 ☐	14:1-31 ☐
43	15:1-34 ☐	16:1—17:24 ☐	18:1-46 ☐	19:1-21 ☐	20:1-43 ☐	21:1—22:53 ☐	2 Kings 1:1-18 ☐
44	2:1—3:27 ☐	4:1-44 ☐	5:1—6:33 ☐	7:1-20 ☐	8:1-29 ☐	9:1-37 ☐	10:1-36 ☐
45	11:1—12:21 ☐	13:1—14:29 ☐	15:1-38 ☐	16:1-20 ☐	17:1-41 ☐	18:1-37 ☐	19:1-37 ☐
46	20:1—21:26 ☐	22:1-20 ☐	23:1-37 ☐	24:1—25:30 ☐	1 Chron. 1:1-54 ☐	2:1—3:24 ☐	4:1—5:26 ☐
47	6:1-81 ☐	7:1-40 ☐	8:1-40 ☐	9:1-44 ☐	10:1—11:47 ☐	12:1-40 ☐	13:1—14:17 ☐
48	15:1—16:43 ☐	17:1-27 ☐	18:1—19:19 ☐	20:1—21:30 ☐	22:1—23:32 ☐	24:1—25:31 ☐	26:1-32 ☐
49	27:1-34 ☐	28:1—29:30 ☐	2 Chron. 1:1-17 ☐	2:1—3:17 ☐	4:1—5:14 ☐	6:1-42 ☐	7:1—8:18 ☐
50	9:1—10:19 ☐	11:1—12:16 ☐	13:1—15:19 ☐	16:1—17:19 ☐	18:1—19:11 ☐	20:1-37 ☐	21:1—22:12 ☐
51	23:1—24:27 ☐	25:1—26:23 ☐	27:1—28:27 ☐	29:1-36 ☐	30:1—31:21 ☐	32:1-33 ☐	33:1—34:33 ☐
52	35:1—36:23 ☐	Ezra 1:1-11 ☐	2:1-70 ☐	3:1—4:24 ☐	5:1—6:22 ☐	7:1-28 ☐	8:1-36 ☐

Reading Schedule for the Recovery Version of the Old Testament with Footnotes

Wk.	Lord's Day	Monday	Tuesday	Wednesday	Thursday	Friday	Saturday
53	9:1—10:44 ☐	Neh. 1:1-11 ☐	2:1—3:32 ☐	4:1—5:19 ☐	6:1-19 ☐	7:1-73 ☐	8:1-18 ☐
54	9:1-20 ☐	9:21-38 ☐	10:1—11:36 ☐	12:1-47 ☐	13:1-31 ☐	Esth. 1:1-22 ☐	2:1—3:15 ☐
55	4:1—5:14 ☐	6:1—7:10 ☐	8:1-17 ☐	9:1—10:3 ☐	Job 1:1-22 ☐	2:1—3:26 ☐	4:1—5:27 ☐
56	6:1—7:21 ☐	8:1—9:35 ☐	10:1—11:20 ☐	12:1—13:28 ☐	14:1—15:35 ☐	16:1—17:16 ☐	18:1—19:29 ☐
57	20:1—21:34 ☐	22:1—23:17 ☐	24:1—25:6 ☐	26:1—27:23 ☐	28:1—29:25 ☐	30:1—31:40 ☐	32:1—33:33 ☐
58	34:1—35:16 ☐	36:1-33 ☐	37:1-24 ☐	38:1-41 ☐	39:1-30 ☐	40:1-24 ☐	41:1-34 ☐
59	42:1-17 ☐	Psa. 1:1-6 ☐	2:1—3:8 ☐	4:1—6:10 ☐	7:1—8:9 ☐	9:1—10:18 ☐	11:1—15:5 ☐
60	16:1—17:15 ☐	18:1-50 ☐	19:1—21:13 ☐	22:1-31 ☐	23:1—24:10 ☐	25:1—27:14 ☐	28:1—30:12 ☐
61	31:1—32:11 ☐	33:1—34:22 ☐	35:1—36:12 ☐	37:1-40 ☐	38:1—39:13 ☐	40:1—41:13 ☐	42:1—43:5 ☐
62	44:1-26 ☐	45:1-17 ☐	46:1—48:14 ☐	49:1—50:23 ☐	51:1—52:9 ☐	53:1—55:23 ☐	56:1—58:11 ☐
63	59:1—61:8 ☐	62:1—64:10 ☐	65:1—67:7 ☐	68:1-35 ☐	69:1—70:5 ☐	71:1—72:20 ☐	73:1—74:23 ☐
64	75:1—77:20 ☐	78:1-72 ☐	79:1—81:16 ☐	82:1—84:12 ☐	85:1—87:7 ☐	88:1—89:52 ☐	90:1—91:16 ☐
65	92:1—94:23 ☐	95:1—97:12 ☐	98:1—101:8 ☐	102:1—103:22 ☐	104:1—105:45 ☐	106:1-48 ☐	107:1-43 ☐
66	108:1—109:31 ☐	110:1—112:10 ☐	113:1—115:18 ☐	116:1—118:29 ☐	119:1-32 ☐	119:33-72 ☐	119:73-120 ☐
67	119:121-176 ☐	120:1—124:8 ☐	125:1—128:6 ☐	129:1—132:18 ☐	133:1—135:21 ☐	136:1—138:8 ☐	139:1—140:13 ☐
68	141:1—144:15 ☐	145:1—147:20 ☐	148:1—150:6 ☐	Prov. 1:1-33 ☐	2:1—3:35 ☐	4:1—5:23 ☐	6:1-35 ☐
69	7:1—8:36 ☐	9:1—10:32 ☐	11:1—12:28 ☐	13:1—14:35 ☐	15:1-33 ☐	16:1-33 ☐	17:1-28 ☐
70	18:1-24 ☐	19:1—20:30 ☐	21:1—22:29 ☐	23:1—35 ☐	24:1—25:28 ☐	26:1—27:27 ☐	28:1—29:27 ☐
71	30:1-33 ☐	31:1-31 ☐	Eccl. 1:1-18 ☐	2:1—3:22 ☐	4:1—5:20 ☐	6:1—7:29 ☐	8:1—9:18 ☐
72	10:1—11:10 ☐	12:1-14 ☐	S.S. 1:1-8 ☐	1:9-17 ☐	2:1-17 ☐	3:1-11 ☐	4:1-8 ☐
73	4:9-16 ☐	5:1-16 ☐	6:1-13 ☐	7:1-13 ☐	8:1-14 ☐	Isa. 1:1-11 ☐	1:12-31 ☐
74	2:1-22 ☐	3:1-26 ☐	4:1-6 ☐	5:1-30 ☐	6:1-13 ☐	7:1-25 ☐	8:1-22 ☐
75	9:1-21 ☐	10:1-34 ☐	11:1—12:6 ☐	13:1-22 ☐	14:1-14 ☐	14:15-32 ☐	15:1—16:14 ☐
76	17:1—18:7 ☐	19:1-25 ☐	20:1—21:17 ☐	22:1-25 ☐	23:1-18 ☐	24:1-23 ☐	25:1-12 ☐
77	26:1-21 ☐	27:1-13 ☐	28:1-29 ☐	29:1-24 ☐	30:1-33 ☐	31:1—32:20 ☐	33:1-24 ☐
78	34:1-17 ☐	35:1-10 ☐	36:1-22 ☐	37:1-38 ☐	38:1—39:8 ☐	40:1-31 ☐	41:1-29 ☐

Reading Schedule for the Recovery Version of the Old Testament with Footnotes

Wk.	Lord's Day	Monday	Tuesday	Wednesday	Thursday	Friday	Saturday
79	42:1-25 ☐	43:1-28 ☐	44:1-28 ☐	45:1-25 ☐	46:1-13 ☐	47:1-15 ☐	48:1-22 ☐
80	49:1-13 ☐	49:14-26 ☐	50:1—51:23 ☐	52:1-15 ☐	53:1-12 ☐	54:1-17 ☐	55:1-13 ☐
81	56:1-12 ☐	57:1-21 ☐	58:1-14 ☐	59:1-21 ☐	60:1-22 ☐	61:1-11 ☐	62:1-12 ☐
82	63:1-19 ☐	64:1-12 ☐	65:1-25 ☐	66:1-24 ☐	Jer. 1:1-19 ☐	2:1-19 ☐	2:20-37 ☐
83	3:1-25 ☐	4:1-31 ☐	5:1-31 ☐	6:1-30 ☐	7:1-34 ☐	8:1-22 ☐	9:1-26 ☐
84	10:1-25 ☐	11:1—12:17 ☐	13:1-27 ☐	14:1-22 ☐	15:1-21 ☐	16:1—17:27 ☐	18:1-23 ☐
85	19:1—20:18 ☐	21:1—22:30 ☐	23:1-40 ☐	24:1—25:38 ☐	26:1—27:22 ☐	28:1—29:32 ☐	30:1-24 ☐
86	31:1-23 ☐	31:24-40 ☐	32:1-44 ☐	33:1-26 ☐	34:1-22 ☐	35:1-19 ☐	36:1-32 ☐
87	37:1-21 ☐	38:1-28 ☐	39:1—40:16 ☐	41:1—42:22 ☐	43:1—44:30 ☐	45:1—46:28 ☐	47:1—48:16 ☐
88	48:17-47 ☐	49:1-22 ☐	49:23-39 ☐	50:1-27 ☐	50:28-46 ☐	51:1-27 ☐	51:28-64 ☐
89	52:1-34 ☐	Lam. 1:1-22 ☐	2:1-22 ☐	3:1-39 ☐	3:40-66 ☐	4:1-22 ☐	5:1-22 ☐
90	Ezek. 1:1-14 ☐	1:15-28 ☐	2:1—3:27 ☐	4:1—5:17 ☐	6:1—7:27 ☐	8:1—9:11 ☐	10:1—11:25 ☐
91	12:1—13:23 ☐	14:1—15:8 ☐	16:1-63 ☐	17:1—18:32 ☐	19:1-14 ☐	20:1-49 ☐	21:1-32 ☐
92	22:1-31 ☐	23:1-49 ☐	24:1-27 ☐	25:1—26:21 ☐	27:1-36 ☐	28:1-26 ☐	29:1—30:26 ☐
93	31:1—32:32 ☐	33:1-33 ☐	34:1-31 ☐	35:1—36:21 ☐	36:22-38 ☐	37:1-28 ☐	38:1—39:29 ☐
94	40:1-27 ☐	40:28-49 ☐	41:1-26 ☐	42:1—43:27 ☐	44:1-31 ☐	45:1-25 ☐	46:1-24 ☐
95	47:1-23 ☐	48:1-35 ☐	Dan. 1:1-21 ☐	2:1-30 ☐	2:31-49 ☐	3:1-30 ☐	4:1-37 ☐
96	5:1-31 ☐	6:1-28 ☐	7:1-12 ☐	7:13-28 ☐	8:1-27 ☐	9:1-27 ☐	10:1-21 ☐
97	11:1-22 ☐	11:23-45 ☐	12:1-13 ☐	Hosea 1:1-11 ☐	2:1-23 ☐	3:1—4:19 ☐	5:1-15 ☐
98	6:1-11 ☐	7:1-16 ☐	8:1-14 ☐	9:1-17 ☐	10:1-15 ☐	11:1-12 ☐	12:1-14 ☐
99	13:1—14:9 ☐	Joel 1:1-20 ☐	2:1-16 ☐	2:17-32 ☐	3:1-21 ☐	Amos 1:1-15 ☐	2:1-16 ☐
100	3:1-15 ☐	4:1—5:27 ☐	6:1—7:17 ☐	8:1—9:15 ☐	Obad. 1-21 ☐	Jonah 1:1-17 ☐	2:1—4:11 ☐
101	Micah 1:1-16 ☐	2:1—3:12 ☐	4:1—5:15 ☐	6:1—7:20 ☐	Nahum 1:1-15 ☐	2:1—3:19 ☐	Hab. 1:1-17 ☐
102	2:1-20 ☐	3:1-19 ☐	Zeph. 1:1-18 ☐	2:1-15 ☐	3:1-20 ☐	Hag. 1:1-15 ☐	2:1-23 ☐
103	Zech. 1:1-21 ☐	2:1-13 ☐	3:1-10 ☐	4:1-14 ☐	5:1—6:15 ☐	7:1—8:23 ☐	9:1-17 ☐
104	10:1—11:17 ☐	12:1—13:9 ☐	14:1-21 ☐	Mal. 1:1-14 ☐	2:1-17 ☐	3:1-18 ☐	4:1-6 ☐

Reading Schedule for the Recovery Version of the New Testament with Footnotes

Wk.	Lord's Day	Monday	Tuesday	Wednesday	Thursday	Friday	Saturday
1	Matt. 1:1-2 ☐	1:3-7 ☐	1:8-17 ☐	1:18-25 ☐	2:1-23 ☐	3:1-6 ☐	3:7-17 ☐
2	4:1-11 ☐	4:12-25 ☐	5:1-4 ☐	5:5-12 ☐	5:13-20 ☐	5:21-26 ☐	5:27-48 ☐
3	6:1-8 ☐	6:9-18 ☐	6:19-34 ☐	7:1-12 ☐	7:13-29 ☐	8:1-13 ☐	8:14-22 ☐
4	8:23-34 ☐	9:1-13 ☐	9:14-17 ☐	9:18-34 ☐	9:35—10:5 ☐	10:6-25 ☐	10:26-42 ☐
5	11:1-15 ☐	11:16-30 ☐	12:1-14 ☐	12:15-32 ☐	12:33-42 ☐	12:43—13:2 ☐	13:3-12 ☐
6	13:13-30 ☐	13:31-43 ☐	13:44-58 ☐	14:1-13 ☐	14:14-21 ☐	14:22-36 ☐	15:1-20 ☐
7	15:21-31 ☐	15:32-39 ☐	16:1-12 ☐	16:13-20 ☐	16:21-28 ☐	17:1-13 ☐	17:14-27 ☐
8	18:1-14 ☐	18:15-22 ☐	18:23-35 ☐	19:1-15 ☐	19:16-30 ☐	20:1-16 ☐	20:17-34 ☐
9	21:1-11 ☐	21:12-22 ☐	21:23-32 ☐	21:33-46 ☐	22:1-22 ☐	22:23-33 ☐	22:34-46 ☐
10	23:1-12 ☐	23:13-39 ☐	24:1-14 ☐	24:15-31 ☐	24:32-51 ☐	25:1-13 ☐	25:14-30 ☐
11	25:31-46 ☐	26:1-16 ☐	26:17-35 ☐	26:36-46 ☐	26:47-64 ☐	26:65-75 ☐	27:1-26 ☐
12	27:27-44 ☐	27:45-56 ☐	27:57—28:15 ☐	28:16-20 ☐	Mark 1:1 ☐	1:2-6 ☐	1:7-13 ☐
13	1:14-28 ☐	1:29-45 ☐	2:1-12 ☐	2:13-28 ☐	3:1-19 ☐	3:20-35 ☐	4:1-25 ☐
14	4:26-41 ☐	5:1-20 ☐	5:21-43 ☐	6:1-29 ☐	6:30-56 ☐	7:1-23 ☐	7:24-37 ☐
15	8:1-26 ☐	8:27—9:1 ☐	9:2-29 ☐	9:30-50 ☐	10:1-16 ☐	10:17-34 ☐	10:35-52 ☐
16	11:1-16 ☐	11:17-33 ☐	12:1-27 ☐	12:28-44 ☐	13:1-13 ☐	13:14-37 ☐	14:1-26 ☐
17	14:27-52 ☐	14:53-72 ☐	15:1-15 ☐	15:16-47 ☐	16:1-8 ☐	16:9-20 ☐	Luke 1:1-4 ☐
18	1:5-25 ☐	1:26-46 ☐	1:47-56 ☐	1:57-80 ☐	2:1-8 ☐	2:9-20 ☐	2:21-39 ☐
19	2:40-52 ☐	3:1-20 ☐	3:21-38 ☐	4:1-13 ☐	4:14-30 ☐	4:31-44 ☐	5:1-26 ☐
20	5:27—6:16 ☐	6:17-38 ☐	6:39-49 ☐	7:1-17 ☐	7:18-23 ☐	7:24-35 ☐	7:36-50 ☐
21	8:1-15 ☐	8:16-25 ☐	8:26-39 ☐	8:40-56 ☐	9:1-17 ☐	9:18-26 ☐	9:27-36 ☐
22	9:37-50 ☐	9:51-62 ☐	10:1-11 ☐	10:12-24 ☐	10:25-37 ☐	10:38-42 ☐	11:1-13 ☐
23	11:14-26 ☐	11:27-36 ☐	11:37-54 ☐	12:1-12 ☐	12:13-21 ☐	12:22-34 ☐	12:35-48 ☐
24	12:49-59 ☐	13:1-9 ☐	13:10-17 ☐	13:18-30 ☐	13:31—14:6 ☐	14:7-14 ☐	14:15-24 ☐
25	14:25-35 ☐	15:1-10 ☐	15:11-21 ☐	15:22-32 ☐	16:1-13 ☐	16:14-22 ☐	16:23-31 ☐
26	17:1-19 ☐	17:20-37 ☐	18:1-14 ☐	18:15-30 ☐	18:31-43 ☐	19:1-10 ☐	19:11-27 ☐

Reading Schedule for the Recovery Version of the New Testament with Footnotes

Wk.	Lord's Day	Monday	Tuesday	Wednesday	Thursday	Friday	Saturday
27	Luke 19:28-48 ☐	20:1-19 ☐	20:20-38 ☐	20:39—21:4 ☐	21:5-27 ☐	21:28-38 ☐	22:1-20 ☐
28	22:21-38 ☐	22:39-54 ☐	22:55-71 ☐	23:1-43 ☐	23:44-56 ☐	24:1-12 ☐	24:13-35 ☐
29	24:36-53 ☐	John 1:1-13 ☐	1:14-18 ☐	1:19-34 ☐	1:35-51 ☐	2:1-11 ☐	2:12-22 ☐
30	2:23—3:13 ☐	3:14-21 ☐	3:22-36 ☐	4:1-14 ☐	4:15-26 ☐	4:27-42 ☐	4:43-54 ☐
31	5:1-16 ☐	5:17-30 ☐	5:31-47 ☐	6:1-15 ☐	6:16-31 ☐	6:32-51 ☐	6:52-71 ☐
32	7:1-9 ☐	7:10-24 ☐	7:25-36 ☐	7:37-52 ☐	7:53—8:11 ☐	8:12-27 ☐	8:28-44 ☐
33	8:45-59 ☐	9:1-13 ☐	9:14-34 ☐	9:35—10:9 ☐	10:10-30 ☐	10:31—11:4 ☐	11:5-22 ☐
34	11:23-40 ☐	11:41-57 ☐	12:1-11 ☐	12:12-24 ☐	12:25-36 ☐	12:37-50 ☐	13:1-11 ☐
35	13:12-30 ☐	13:31-38 ☐	14:1-6 ☐	14:7-20 ☐	14:21-31 ☐	15:1-11 ☐	15:12-27 ☐
36	16:1-15 ☐	16:16-33 ☐	17:1-5 ☐	17:6-13 ☐	17:14-24 ☐	17:25—18:11 ☐	18:12-27 ☐
37	18:28-40 ☐	19:1-16 ☐	19:17-30 ☐	19:31-42 ☐	20:1-13 ☐	20:14-18 ☐	20:19-22 ☐
38	20:23-31 ☐	21:1-14 ☐	21:15-22 ☐	21:23-25 ☐	Acts 1:1-8 ☐	1:9-14 ☐	1:15-26 ☐
39	2:1-13 ☐	2:14-21 ☐	2:22-36 ☐	2:37-41 ☐	2:42-47 ☐	3:1-18 ☐	3:19—4:22 ☐
40	4:23-37 ☐	5:1-16 ☐	5:17-32 ☐	5:33-42 ☐	6:1—7:1 ☐	7:2-29 ☐	7:30-60 ☐
41	8:1-13 ☐	8:14-25 ☐	8:26-40 ☐	9:1-19 ☐	9:20-43 ☐	10:1-16 ☐	10:17-33 ☐
42	10:34-48 ☐	11:1-18 ☐	11:19-30 ☐	12:1-25 ☐	13:1-12 ☐	13:13-43 ☐	13:44—14:5 ☐
43	14:6-28 ☐	15:1-12 ☐	15:13-34 ☐	15:35—16:5 ☐	16:6-18 ☐	16:19-40 ☐	17:1-18 ☐
44	17:19-34 ☐	18:1-17 ☐	18:18-28 ☐	19:1-20 ☐	19:21-41 ☐	20:1-12 ☐	20:13-38 ☐
45	21:1-14 ☐	21:15-26 ☐	21:27-40 ☐	22:1-21 ☐	22:22-29 ☐	22:30—23:11 ☐	23:12-15 ☐
46	23:16-30 ☐	23:31—24:21 ☐	24:22—25:5 ☐	25:6-27 ☐	26:1-13 ☐	26:14-32 ☐	27:1-26 ☐
47	27:27—28:10 ☐	28:11-22 ☐	28:23-31 ☐	Rom 1:1-2 ☐	1:3-7 ☐	1:8-17 ☐	1:18-25 ☐
48	1:26—2:10 ☐	2:11-29 ☐	3:1-20 ☐	3:21-31 ☐	4:1-12 ☐	4:13-25 ☐	5:1-11 ☐
49	5:12-17 ☐	5:18—6:5 ☐	6:6-11 ☐	6:12-23 ☐	7:1-12 ☐	7:13-25 ☐	8:1-2 ☐
50	8:3-6 ☐	8:7-13 ☐	8:14-25 ☐	8:26-39 ☐	9:1-18 ☐	9:19—10:3 ☐	10:4-15 ☐
51	10:16—11:10 ☐	11:11-22 ☐	11:23-36 ☐	12:1-3 ☐	12:4-21 ☐	13:1-14 ☐	14:1-12 ☐
52	14:13-23 ☐	15:1-13 ☐	15:14-33 ☐	16:1-5 ☐	16:6-24 ☐	16:25-27 ☐	1 Cor. 1:1-4 ☐

Reading Schedule for the Recovery Version of the New Testament with Footnotes

Wk.	Lord's Day	Monday	Tuesday	Wednesday	Thursday	Friday	Saturday
53	1 Cor. 1:5-9 ☐	1:10-17 ☐	1:18-31 ☐	2:1-5 ☐	2:6-10 ☐	2:11-16 ☐	3:1-9 ☐
54	3:10-13 ☐	3:14-23 ☐	4:1-9 ☐	4:10-21 ☐	5:1-13 ☐	6:1-11 ☐	6:12-20 ☐
55	7:1-16 ☐	7:17-24 ☐	7:25-40 ☐	8:1-13 ☐	9:1-15 ☐	9:16-27 ☐	10:1-4 ☐
56	10:5-13 ☐	10:14-33 ☐	11:1-6 ☐	11:7-16 ☐	11:17-26 ☐	11:27-34 ☐	12:1-11 ☐
57	12:12-22 ☐	12:23-31 ☐	13:1-13 ☐	14:1-12 ☐	14:13-25 ☐	14:26-33 ☐	14:34-40 ☐
58	15:1-19 ☐	15:20-28 ☐	15:29-34 ☐	15:35-49 ☐	15:50-58 ☐	16:1-9 ☐	16:10-24 ☐
59	2 Cor. 1:1-4 ☐	1:5-14 ☐	1:15-22 ☐	1:23—2:11 ☐	2:12-17 ☐	3:1-6 ☐	3:7-11 ☐
60	3:12-18 ☐	4:1-6 ☐	4:7-12 ☐	4:13-18 ☐	5:1-8 ☐	5:9-15 ☐	5:16-21 ☐
61	6:1-13 ☐	6:14—7:4 ☐	7:5-16 ☐	8:1-15 ☐	8:16-24 ☐	9:1-15 ☐	10:1-6 ☐
62	10:7-18 ☐	11:1-15 ☐	11:16-33 ☐	12:1-10 ☐	12:11-21 ☐	13:1-10 ☐	13:11-14 ☐
63	Gal. 1:1-5 ☐	1:6-14 ☐	1:15-24 ☐	2:1-13 ☐	2:14-21 ☐	3:1-4 ☐	3:5-14 ☐
64	3:15-22 ☐	3:23-29 ☐	4:1-7 ☐	4:8-20 ☐	4:21-31 ☐	5:1-12 ☐	5:13-21 ☐
65	5:22-26 ☐	6:1-10 ☐	6:11-15 ☐	6:16-18 ☐	Eph. 1:1-3 ☐	1:4-6 ☐	1:7-10 ☐
66	1:11-14 ☐	1:15-18 ☐	1:19-23 ☐	2:1-5 ☐	2:6-10 ☐	2:11-14 ☐	2:15-18 ☐
67	2:19-22 ☐	3:1-7 ☐	3:8-13 ☐	3:14-18 ☐	3:19-21 ☐	4:1-4 ☐	4:5-10 ☐
68	4:11-16 ☐	4:17-24 ☐	4:25-32 ☐	5:1-10 ☐	5:11-21 ☐	5:22-26 ☐	5:27-33 ☐
69	6:1-9 ☐	6:10-14 ☐	6:15-18 ☐	6:19-24 ☐	Phil. 1:1-7 ☐	1:8-18 ☐	1:19-26 ☐
70	1:27—2:4 ☐	2:5-11 ☐	2:12-16 ☐	2:17-30 ☐	3:1-6 ☐	3:7-11 ☐	3:12-16 ☐
71	3:17-21 ☐	4:1-9 ☐	4:10-23 ☐	Col. 1:1-8 ☐	1:9-13 ☐	1:14-23 ☐	1:24-29 ☐
72	2:1-7 ☐	2:8-15 ☐	2:16-23 ☐	3:1-4 ☐	3:5-15 ☐	3:16-25 ☐	4:1-18 ☐
73	1 Thes. 1:1-3 ☐	1:4-10 ☐	2:1-12 ☐	2:13—3:5 ☐	3:6-13 ☐	4:1-10 ☐	4:11—5:11 ☐
74	5:12-28 ☐	2 Thes. 1:1-12 ☐	2:1-17 ☐	3:1-18 ☐	1 Tim. 1:1-2 ☐	1:3-4 ☐	1:5-14 ☐
75	1:15-20 ☐	2:1-7 ☐	2:8-15 ☐	3:1-13 ☐	3:14—4:5 ☐	4:6-16 ☐	5:1-25 ☐
76	6:1-10 ☐	6:11-21 ☐	2 Tim. 1:1-10 ☐	1:11-18 ☐	2:1-15 ☐	2:16-26 ☐	3:1-13 ☐
77	3:14—4:8 ☐	4:9-22 ☐	Titus 1:1-4 ☐	1:5-16 ☐	2:1-15 ☐	3:1-8 ☐	3:9-15 ☐
78	Philem. 1:1-11 ☐	1:12-25 ☐	Heb. 1:1-2 ☐	1:3-5 ☐	1:6-14 ☐	2:1-9 ☐	2:10-18 ☐

Reading Schedule for the Recovery Version of the New Testament with Footnotes

Wk.	Lord's Day	Monday	Tuesday	Wednesday	Thursday	Friday	Saturday
79	Heb. 3:1-6 ☐	3:7-19 ☐	4:1-9 ☐	4:10-13 ☐	4:14-16 ☐	5:1-10 ☐	5:11—6:3 ☐
80	6:4-8 ☐	6:9-20 ☐	7:1-10 ☐	7:11-28 ☐	8:1-6 ☐	8:7-13 ☐	9:1-4 ☐
81	9:5-14 ☐	9:15-28 ☐	10:1-18 ☐	10:19-28 ☐	10:29-39 ☐	11:1-6 ☐	11:7-19 ☐
82	11:20-31 ☐	11:32-40 ☐	12:1-2 ☐	12:3-13 ☐	12:14-17 ☐	12:18-26 ☐	12:27-29 ☐
83	13:1-7 ☐	13:8-12 ☐	13:13-15 ☐	13:16-25 ☐	James 1:1-8 ☐	1:9-18 ☐	1:19-27 ☐
84	2:1-13 ☐	2:14-26 ☐	3:1-18 ☐	4:1-10 ☐	4:11-17 ☐	5:1-12 ☐	5:13-20 ☐
85	1 Pet. 1:1-2 ☐	1:3-4 ☐	1:5 ☐	1:6-9 ☐	1:10-12 ☐	1:13-17 ☐	1:18-25 ☐
86	2:1-3 ☐	2:4-8 ☐	2:9-17 ☐	2:18-25 ☐	3:1-13 ☐	3:14-22 ☐	4:1-6 ☐
87	4:7-16 ☐	4:17-19 ☐	5:1-4 ☐	5:5-9 ☐	5:10-14 ☐	2 Pet. 1:1-2 ☐	1:3-4 ☐
88	1:5-8 ☐	1:9-11 ☐	1:12-18 ☐	1:19-21 ☐	2:1-3 ☐	2:4-11 ☐	2:12-22 ☐
89	3:1-6 ☐	3:7-9 ☐	3:10-12 ☐	3:13-15 ☐	3:16 ☐	3:17-18 ☐	1 John 1:1-2 ☐
90	1:3-4 ☐	1:5 ☐	1:6 ☐	1:7 ☐	1:8-10 ☐	2:1-2 ☐	2:3-11 ☐
91	2:12-14 ☐	2:15-19 ☐	2:20-23 ☐	2:24-27 ☐	2:28-29 ☐	3:1-5 ☐	3:6-10 ☐
92	3:11-18 ☐	3:19-24 ☐	4:1-6 ☐	4:7-11 ☐	4:12-15 ☐	4:16—5:3 ☐	5:4-13 ☐
93	5:14-17 ☐	5:18-21 ☐	2 John 1:1-3 ☐	1:4-9 ☐	1:10-13 ☐	3 John 1:1-6 ☐	1:7-14 ☐
94	Jude 1:1-4 ☐	1:5-10 ☐	1:11-19 ☐	1:20-25 ☐	Rev. 1:1-3 ☐	1:4-6 ☐	1:7-11 ☐
95	1:12-13 ☐	1:14-16 ☐	1:17-20 ☐	2:1-6 ☐	2:7 ☐	2:8-9 ☐	2:10-11 ☐
96	2:12-14 ☐	2:15-17 ☐	2:18-23 ☐	2:24-29 ☐	3:1-3 ☐	3:4-6 ☐	3:7-9 ☐
97	3:10-13 ☐	3:14-18 ☐	3:19-22 ☐	4:1-5 ☐	4:6-7 ☐	4:8-11 ☐	5:1-6 ☐
98	5:7-14 ☐	6:1-8 ☐	6:9-17 ☐	7:1-8 ☐	7:9-17 ☐	8:1-6 ☐	8:7-12 ☐
99	8:13—9:11 ☐	9:12-21 ☐	10:1-4 ☐	10:5-11 ☐	11:1-4 ☐	11:5-14 ☐	11:15-19 ☐
100	12:1-4 ☐	12:5-9 ☐	12:10-18 ☐	13:1-10 ☐	13:11-18 ☐	14:1-5 ☐	14:6-12 ☐
101	14:13-20 ☐	15:1-8 ☐	16:1-12 ☐	16:13-21 ☐	17:1-6 ☐	17:7-18 ☐	18:1-8 ☐
102	18:9—19:4 ☐	19:5-10 ☐	19:11-16 ☐	19:17-21 ☐	20:1-6 ☐	20:7-10 ☐	20:11-15 ☐
103	21:1 ☐	21:2 ☐	21:3-8 ☐	21:9-13 ☐	21:14-18 ☐	21:19-21 ☐	21:22-27 ☐
104	22:1 ☐	22:2 ☐	22:3-11 ☐	22:12-15 ☐	22:16-17 ☐	22:18-21 ☐	

1st Day: CONFERENCE 15-5-20

Sang Hymn 132 & 946

They asked d brother 3 on that is
happenin now relates God Lord's comin
Gods Sovereignty — Gave free voice
Pple will ask why did God allow pple to suffer

God Remain Hidden

God has a throne next'
G: Remove
Rom:

We are in d age of GODs
INTESI   ION .

Act 1   Hymn 381, 474
2nd Day Conference
Started 1 Cor 729 etc 10 vs 11-12
Also Matt 24 23 & vs 14 very
essential in dis last days —
We preach d divine truth
form Matthew to Revelation
nations — peoples
The Preaching of gospel of d
kingdom has already been Nation

Week 7 — Day 4　　　　Today's verses

1 Cor. But to the rest I say, I, not the Lord, If
7:12　any brother has an unbelieving wife
and she consents to dwell with him,
he must not leave her.

25　Now concerning virgins I have no
commandment of the Lord, but I give
my opinion as one who has been
shown mercy by the Lord to be faithful.

_____
Date

Week 7 — Day 5　　　　Today's verses

1 Cor. But she is more blessed if she so re-
7:40　mains, according to my opinion; but
I think that I also have the Spirit of
God.

6:17　But he who is joined to the Lord is
one spirit.

_____
Date

Week 7 — Day 6　　　　Today's verses

1 Cor. But to the married I charge, not I but
7:10　the Lord, A wife must not be separated from *her* husband.

2:13　Which things also we speak, not in
words taught by human wisdom but
in words taught by the Spirit, inter-
preting spiritual things with spiritual
words.

_____
Date

Week 7 — Day 1　　　　Today's verses

Amos Surely the Lord Jehovah will not do
3:7　anything unless He reveals His secret
to His servants the prophets.

2 Pet. Knowing this first, that no prophecy
1:20-21　of Scripture is of one's own interpretation; for no prophecy was ever borne
by the will of man, but men spoke
from God while being borne by the
Holy Spirit.

_____
Date

Week 7 — Day 2　　　　Today's verses

Deut. A Prophet will Jehovah your God raise
18:15　up for you from your midst, from
among your brothers, like me; you
shall listen to Him.

18　A Prophet will I raise up for them from
the midst of their brothers like you;
and I will put My words in His mouth,
and He will speak to them all that I
command Him.

_____
Date

Week 7 — Day 3　　　　Today's verses

John For He whom God has sent speaks the
3:34　words of God, for He gives the Spirit
not by measure.

8:28　...I do nothing from Myself, but as My
Father has taught Me, I speak these
things.

Rev. ...His name is called the Word of
19:13　God.

_____
Date

1948 Isreal reformation
1967 Jerusalem   Matt 24?
picture of what God is doing
in this economy

Where are we in church
history 1st Act 2 read very import
(Philadelphia became Laodicia)
The white horse in revelati
b d spread
b d preaching of d gospel
1. World ultimate move on d eath
2.

3rd The Lord ultimate recovery
    USA is d superpower no mor
Soviet Union. Everybody in d
whole world people speak English
D high peack English has become
d divine revelation of d Church
life (d. recovery)
    We have inherited dis ultimate
which is d RECOVERY U so
much is required from U so
    Lampstand this is what God
is after filled c d Triune God
consumate of ages et
May we be faithful to
Gods Testimony on eath.

Week 8 — Day 4   Today's verses

Gal. Christ has redeemed us out of the
3:13 curse of the law, having become a
curse on our behalf; because it is
written, "Cursed is everyone hanging
on a tree."

29 And if you are of Christ, then you are
Abraham's seed, heirs according to
promise.

_____
Date

Week 8 — Day 1   Today's verses

Deut. And if in a man there is a sin, a cause
21:22-23 worthy of death, and he is put to death,
and you hang him on a tree; his corpse
shall not remain overnight on the tree,
but you must bury him on that day.
For he who is hanged is accursed of
God…

Acts The God of our fathers has raised Jesus,
5:30 whom you slew by hanging Him on
a tree.

_____
Date

Week 8 — Day 5   Today's verses

Gen. And I will bless those who bless you…;
12:3 and in you all the families of the earth
will be blessed.

Col. Giving thanks to the Father, who has
1:12 qualified you for a share of the allotted portion of the saints in the light.

2 Cor. And the Lord is the Spirit; and where
3:17 the Spirit of the Lord is, there is freedom.

_____
Date

Week 8 — Day 2   Today's verses

Rom. For if, by the offense of the one, death
5:17 reigned through the one, much more
those who receive the abundance of
grace and of the gift of righteousness
will reign in life through the One, Jesus
Christ.

6:23 For the wages of sin is death, but the
gift of God is eternal life in Christ Jesus
our Lord.

_____
Date

Week 8 — Day 6   Today's verses

Gal. This only I wish to learn from you,
3:2 Did you receive the Spirit out of the
works of law or out of the hearing of
faith?

5 He therefore who bountifully supplies
to you the Spirit and does works of
power among you, does He do it out
of the works of law or out of the hearing of faith?

_____
Date

Week 8 — Day 3   Today's verses

1 Pet. Who Himself bore up our sins in His
2:24 body on the tree, in order that we, having died to sins, might live to righteousness; by whose bruise you were
healed.

Mark And at the ninth hour Jesus cried with
15:34 a loud voice, Eloi, Eloi, lama sabachthani? which is interpreted, My God,
My God, why have You forsaken Me?

_____
Date

3rd Msge Question & Answer

include experience Christ a
all inclusive extensive Christ

Week 9 — Day 4	Today's verses	Week 9 — Day 5	Today's verses	Week 9 — Day 6	Today's verses
Psa. 48:2	Beautiful in elevation, the joy of the whole earth, is Mount Zion, the sides of the north, the city of the great King.	Deut. 12:15	Yet you may slaughter and eat meat within all your gates…according to the blessing of Jehovah your God which He has given you.…	Col. 1:18	And He is the Head of the Body, the church; He is the beginning, the First-born from the dead, that He Himself might have the first place in all things.
11-12	Let Mount Zion rejoice; let the daughters of Judah exult because of Your judgments. Walk about Zion, and go around her; count her towers.	16:16	Three times a year all your males shall appear before Jehovah your God in the place which He will choose.…And they shall not appear before Jehovah empty-handed.	3:11	Where there cannot be Greek and Jew, circumcision and uncircumcision, barbarian, Scythian, slave, free man, but Christ is all and in all.

_____
Date

_____
Date

_____
Date

Week 9 — Day 1	Today's verses	Week 9 — Day 2	Today's verses	Week 9 — Day 3	Today's verses
Deut. 12:5-7	But to the place which Jehovah your God will choose out of all your tribes to put His name, to His habitation, shall you seek, and there shall you go. And there you shall bring your burnt offerings and your sacrifices,…and there you shall eat before Jehovah your God, and you and your households shall rejoice in all your undertakings, in which Jehovah your God has blessed you.	Rev. 1:11	Saying, What you see write in a scroll and send it to the seven churches: to Ephesus and to Smyrna and to Pergamos and to Thyatira and to Sardis and to Philadelphia and to Laodicea.	1 Cor. 1:2	To the church of God which is in Corinth, to those who have been sanctified in Christ Jesus,…with all those who call upon the name of our Lord Jesus Christ in every place…
		Matt. 18:20	For where there are two or three gathered into My name, there am I in their midst.	2 Chron. 6:5-6	…I have not chosen a city out of all the tribes of Israel to build a house for My name that it might be there;…but I have chosen Jerusalem that My name might be there…

_____
Date

_____
Date

_____
Date

J. Church In Bridgewood

Meeting ID: 872-6091-9431

PW :- 127-414

Sisters Mting.

Week 10 — Day 4 — Today's verses

Col. 1:18 — And He is the Head of the Body, the church; He is the beginning, the First-born from the dead, that He Himself might have the first place in all things.

3:10-11 — And have put on the new man...where there cannot be Greek and Jew, circumcision and uncircumcision, barbarian, Scythian, slave, free man, but Christ is all and in all.

Date

Week 10 — Day 5 — Today's verses

1 Cor. 1:30 — But of Him you are in Christ Jesus, who became wisdom to us from God: both righteousness and sanctification and redemption.

1 John 4:2 — In this you know the Spirit of God: Every spirit which confesses that Jesus Christ has come in the flesh is of God.

Date

Week 10 — Day 6 — Today's verses

Jude 3 — Beloved, while using all diligence to write to you concerning our common salvation, I...exhort you to earnestly contend for the faith once for all delivered to the saints.

20-21 — But you, beloved, building up yourselves upon your most holy faith, praying in the Holy Spirit, keep yourselves in the love of God, awaiting the mercy of our Lord Jesus Christ unto eternal life.

Date

Week 10 — Day 1 — Today's verses

Deut. 13:3-4 — You shall not listen to the words of that prophet or to that dreamer of dreams; for Jehovah your God is testing you in order to know whether you love Jehovah your God with all your heart and with all your soul. You shall follow Jehovah your God; and you shall fear Him, keep His commandments, listen to His voice, serve Him, and hold fast to Him.

Date

Week 10 — Day 2 — Today's verses

Eph. 4:14 — That we may be no longer little children tossed by waves and carried about by every wind of teaching in the sleight of men, in craftiness with a view to a system of error.

1 Tim. 1:3-4 — Even as I exhorted you...to remain in Ephesus in order that you might charge certain ones not to teach different things...which produce questionings rather than God's economy, which is in faith.

Date

Week 10 — Day 3 — Today's verses

1 Cor. 4:17 — Because of this I have sent Timothy to you, who is my beloved and faithful child in the Lord, who will remind you of my ways which are in Christ, even as I teach everywhere in every church.

11:16 — But if anyone seems to be contentious, we do not have such a custom of being so, neither the churches of God.

Date

Job 28:28 And unto man
He said, Behold, D FEAR of the
LORD is WISDOM; And
TO DEPART FROM EVIL is UNDERSTANDING
(Amen)

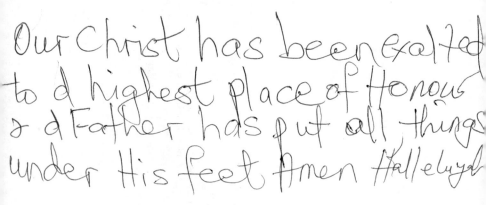

Our Christ has been exalted
to d highest place of Honour
& d Father has put all things
under His feet Amen Halleluyah

Christ is d Reality
Of all d Shadows
We see in d book of Cols
what Christ b— we see
Colosian in Ephsens & in Philippia
Col 1:16-9 & vs

Week 11 — Day 4   Today's verses

Deut.
17:18-19

And when he sits on the throne of his kingdom, he shall write out for himself a copy of this law in a book, out of *that which is* before the Levitical priests. And it shall be with him, and he shall read in it all the days of his life, in order that he may learn to fear Jehovah his God by keeping all the words of this law and these statutes and doing them.

Date

Week 11 — Day 5   Today's verses

Deut.
12:19

Be careful that you do not forsake the Levite all your days upon the earth.

1 Cor.
16:1-2

Now concerning the collection for the saints, just as I directed the churches of Galatia, so you also do. On the first day of the week each one of you should lay aside in store to himself whatever he may have been prospered, that no collections be made when I come.

Date

Week 11 — Day 6   Today's verses

Deut.
25:13-15

You shall not have in your bag differing weights.... You shall not have in your house differing measures....A full and righteous weight...and a full and righteous measure you shall have... that your days may be extended upon the land which Jehovah your God is giving you.

Gal.
6:10

...Let us do what is good toward all, but especially toward those of the household of the faith.

Date

Week 11 — Day 1   Today's verses

1 Cor.
10:1

For I do not want you to be ignorant, brothers, that all our fathers were under the cloud, and all passed through the sea.

6

Now these things occurred as examples to us, that we should not be ones who lust after evil things, even as they also lusted.

Date

Week 11 — Day 2   Today's verses

Rev.
4:2

Immediately I was in spirit; and behold, there was a throne set in heaven, and upon the throne *there was* One sitting.

5:6

And I saw in the midst of the throne and of the four living creatures and in the midst of the elders a Lamb standing as having *just* been slain, having seven horns and seven eyes, which are the seven Spirits of God sent forth into all the earth.

Date

Week 11 — Day 3   Today's verses

Deut.
16:18

You shall appoint for yourself judges and officers in all your cities which Jehovah your God is giving you, according to your tribes; and they shall judge the people with righteous judgment.

33:8

And concerning Levi he said, May Your Thummim and Urim be with Your faithful man...

Date